ACCA - ACCOUNTANT IN BUSINESS

ACCOUNTANT IN BUSINESS

QUESTION BANK

Second edition July 2008

ISBN 978-1-84808-001-0

Published by

Get Through Guides Ltd.
The Technocentre,
Coventry University Technology Park,
Puma Way,
Coventry
CV1 2TT

Website: www.GetThroughGuides.com
Email: info@GetThroughGuides.com

INDEX

About the paper

The syllabus is assessed by a two hour paper-based or computer-based examination. Questions will assess all parts of the syllabus and will test knowledge and some comprehension or application of this knowledge. The examination will consist of 40 two marks questions, and 10 one mark questions

About the GTG - Question Bank

This question bank of 350 questions covers all important topics of the syllabus. The solution bank provides both the correct answer as well as supporting explanations to enhance your understanding of the subject.

The question bank follows the exam pattern exactly so that the students are well prepared for exam conditions for both paper-based and computer-based exams (CBE). The detailed explanations ensure that students understand how the answers are arrived at.

The question bank includes:
- Multiple choice questions
- Multiple response questions
- Multiple response matching questions
- Practise mock exam

QUESTION BANK

MULTIPLE CHOICE QUESTIONS

1   Which of the following is not an example of an external stakeholder?
    A   A government
    B   A customer
    C   An environmental pressure group
    D   A trade union

                                                                                (2 marks)

2   Which of the following statements is incorrect?
    (i)   The informal organisation influences the relationships between employees.
    (ii)   Not all organisations have informal organisation.
    (iii)   The informal organisation stands in direct contrast to the formal organisation.
    (iv)   The informal organisation does not exist simultaneously with the formal organisation.

    A   (i) and (iv)
    B   (ii) and (iii)
    C   (iv)
    D   (ii) and (iv)

                                                                                (2 marks)

3   Which level in the Anthony hierarchy is responsible for setting the policies and procedures that will enable an organisation to meet its long-term objectives?
    A   Management level
    B   Strategic level
    C   Operational level

                                                                                (1 mark)

4   Which of the following statements is incorrect in the context of Charles Handy's four cultural stereotypes?
    A   Role culture has well-established rules and procedures
    B   Performance is judged by results in task culture
    C   Power culture encourages team approach in the organisation
    D   Personal culture is shaped by the interests of individuals

                                                                                (2 marks)

5   Sun Ltd manufactures different types of machines and industrial equipment and sells them across the USA, Europe and Asia. Which organisational structure is it most likely to use?
    A   Divisional structure
    B   Product structure
    C   Matrix structure
    D   Geographical structure

                                                                                (2 marks)

6   Which one of the following most accurately describes the 'non-executive' director?
    A   A member of the board of directors who does not take an active role in managing the company
    B   A member of the board of directors who takes an active role in managing the company
    C   A former director who is associated with the company after his retirement
    D   A member of the board of directors who takes no part in the company's affairs

                                                                                (2 marks)

7   Which of the following statements is incorrect with respect to the attributes of good quality information?

- (i)   Information should not only provide the data / details that are needed but also those that may be of interest to the user
- (ii)   Information that is not up-to-date is of no use in the decision making process
- (III)   The cost of obtaining the Information can be higher than the benefits derived from using It
- (iv)   Information should suit the requirements of the user

    A   (ii) and (iii)
    B   (i) and (iv)
    C   (ii) and (iv)
    D   (i) and (iii)

(2 marks)

8   Decentralisation helps to empower the staff to address any operational problems and respond to changes in the external environment. Is this statement true or false?

    A   True
    B   False

(1 mark)

9   What is meant by the grapevine?

    A   The way unofficial information is communicated to employees
    B   A characteristic of the formal organisation
    C   An informal communication network
    D   Social relationships and behavioural norms

(2 marks)

10   Which of the following statements is incorrect with respect to the roles of the chair and secretary of a committee?

    A   The main role of the secretary is to support the chair during committee meetings
    B   The chair should intervene in the case of disputes or clashes between committee members
    C   The secretary is responsible for preparing the minutes of the committee meetings
    D   The chair is responsible for communicating the committee decisions to its members

(2 marks)

11   Why do organisations need to maintain appropriate corporate governance standards?

    A   To ensure that business risk is minimised
    B   To ensure that companies do not affect the environment
    C   To ensure that the minimum regulatory requirements are met
    D   To ensure the organisation acts in the best interests of its shareholders

(2 marks)

12   Which of the following is a potential advantage of centralisation?

    A   Faster moving and more flexible organisation
    B   More accountability at lower levels
    C   Teamwork and cooperation amongst employees
    D   Greater efficiency, consistency and uniformity across the organisation

(2 marks)

13   Which of the following is a potential advantage of an informal organisation for a business organisation?

    A   Teamwork and cooperation
    B   The "grapevine effect"
    C   Escape from formal procedures and systems
    D   Personal and social relationships among employees

(2 marks)

14   Which of the following is the main reason why accountants should behave ethically?

- (i)   To follow the code of ethics and conduct laid down by accounting bodies
- (ii)   To protect the interests of shareholders and creditors
- (iii)   To maintain objectivity in all dealings with employees and outside parties
- (iv)   To ensure compliance with organisational strategy, mission and vision

    A   (i), (ii) and (iv)
    B   (i) and (ii)
    C   (iii) and (iv)
    D   (i), (ii) and (iii)

(2 marks)

15 The word "limited" is used in the case of private limited companies because their ownership is not open to the public and is restricted to a lower number of owners than public limited companies. Is this statement true or false?

    A   True

    B   False

    (1 mark)

16 Which of the following is a disadvantage of a scalar chain?

    A   Each employee has only one boss

    B   It results in a slow moving and rigid organisation

    C   A manager has authority over subordinates only in his / her scalar chain

    D   All of the above

    (2 marks)

17 According to Charles Handy's four cultural stereotypes, which of the following organisations would adopt a personal culture?

    A   A large bank

    B   A university

    C   An NGO

    D   A public sector organisation

    (2 marks)

18 Which of the following two stakeholder groups of an organisation are most likely to have conflicting objectives?

    A   Customers and shareholders

    B   Bankers and suppliers

    C   Managers and employees

    D   Government and pressure groups

    (2 marks)

19 Which of the following is an advantage of a committee?

    A   Creation of new ideas

    B   Quick decision-making

    C   Divided responsibility

    D   None of the above

    (2 marks)

20 Which of the following is one of the main objectives of the IFAC?

    A   To develop ethical standards and guidance for use by professional accountants

    B   To develop a single set of high quality, enforceable and global accounting standards

    C   To be a leader in the development of a global accountancy profession

    D   None of the above

    (2 marks)

21 What is meant by the marketing mix?

    A   The use of different advertising and publicity tools

    B   The combination of low price and high quality to achieve greater sales

    C   The mix of different types of products marketed by the organisation

    D   The tactics of price, place, product and promotion

    (2 marks)

22 The informal organisation has no influence on the way employees interact formally. Is this statement true or false?

    A   True

    B   False

    (1 mark)

23 Which of the following best describes the role of the marketing function in an organisation?
(i) To ascertain the current and future needs of customers
(ii) To maximise sales volume
(iii) To deliver products / services to meet the needs and demands of customers

A (i) and (ii)
B (ii) and (iii)
C (i) and (iii)
D (i), (ii) and (iii)

(2 marks)

24 The Sarbanes Oxley regulations are designed to enhance and regulate which aspect of an organisation's functioning?
A Calculation and mitigation of tax liability
B Promotion of health and safety at workplace
C Corporate governance and financial reporting
D Compliance with data protection and security

(2 marks)

25 A university is an example of which type of organisation?
A A public sector organisation
B A non-governmental organisation
C A cooperative
D A not-for-profit organisation

(2 marks)

26 Which of the following best describes business ethics?
A Strict compliance with company policies and procedures
B Impact of organisation's decisions on the society
C Moral rules and principles within business context
D Meeting public expectations of professional conduct

(2 marks)

27 Which of the following statements is correct with respect to best practices in effective corporate governance?
A The audit committee members are typically executive directors
B Non-executive directors scrutinise the performance of management
C The public oversight committee reviews internal control systems
D The remuneration committee determines the salary structure of managers

(2 marks)

28 Which of the following stakeholder groups has a special interest in the organisation's continued existence and prosperity?
A Internal stakeholders
B External stakeholders
C Connected stakeholders

(1 mark)

29 Which of the following best describes the role of the purchasing department?
(i) To procure goods at the lowest prices
(ii) To ensure the correct quantities of goods are available for production
(iii) To procure goods in the shortest time
(iv) To ensure the correct quality of goods are available for production

A (i) and (iii)
B (ii) and (iv)
C (i), (ii) and (iii)
D (i), (ii), (iii) and (iv)

(2 marks)

30 If an organisation has a strategy of keeping a particular stakeholder satisfied, according to Mendelow's stakeholder mapping matrix, which of the following is true for that stakeholder?

A   High interest-high power

B   Low interest-low power

C   High interest-low power

D   Low interest-high power

            (2 marks)

31 Ethical behaviour is not in the long-term interests of business organisations. Is this statement true or false?

A   True

B   False

            (1 mark)

32 "Nature Care" is an environmental pressure group that closely follows Makjem Ltd's operations to ensure that it doesn't pollute the surrounding environment. According to Mendelow's stakeholder mapping matrix, which type of relationship should Makjem have with "Nature Care"?

A   Keep satisfied

B   Minimal effort

C   Key player

D   Keep informed

            (2 marks)

33 Which of the following statements is incorrect?

A   A tall organisation has a relatively wide span of control for each manager

B   A flat organisation has fewer managerial layers

C   A much greater level of independence is given to each employee in a flat organisation

D   A tall organisation has many managerial layers

            (2 marks)

34 In the context of Hofstede's five cultural dimensions, what does the low power distance index indicate?

A   High value for individuality and individual rights

B   Low level of gender differentiation and discrimination

C   Low tolerance for uncertainty and ambiguity

D   Greater equality between different levels of society

            (2 marks)

35 Which of the following are the characteristics of operational information?

A   Quantitative, relevant to short term, obtained from internal sources

B   Mostly quantitative, relevant to short and medium term, obtained mainly from internal sources

C   Both quantitative and qualitative, relevant to long term, obtained from both internal and external sources

            (1 mark)

36 What does Edgar Schein label as the main determinant of organisational culture?

A   The set of shared, taken-for-granted assumptions

B   The organisation's environment

C   The views and feelings of employees

D   Leadership and management style

            (2 marks)

37 Which of the following systems takes data mainly from internal sources and converts it into information in the form of summary, detailed or exception reports?

A   A decision support system

B   A management information system

C   A transaction processing system

D   An office automation system

            (2 marks)

38 Word processing software and spreadsheets which are used to improve the efficiency of common administrative tasks, such as creating business documents, are examples of which of the following?

A   A transaction processing system

B   A management information system

C   An office automation system

D   A decision support system

            (2 marks)

39 FinBank Ltd has an organisational structure which is based on its individual customers and corporate customers. Which type of organisational structure does FinBank have?
A   A departmental structure
B   A divisional structure
C   A product structure
D   A functional structure

(2 marks)

40 As organisations grow in size and complexity, the need arises for direction and management to be separated. Is this statement true or false?
A   True
B   False

(1 mark)

41 Which of the following is formed for a particular purpose on a permanent basis?
A   Joint committee
B   Steering committee
C   Ad hoc committee
D   Standing committee

(2 marks)

42 A regulatory accounting body is an example of what type of an organisation?
A   Commercial
B   Not for profit
C   Public sector
D   Non governmental

(2 marks)

43 An organisation's culture influences its modes of operating. Is this statement true or false?
A   True
B   False

(1 mark)

44 Organisations need to take account of their _____ objectives through analysis of the needs of internal, connected and external stakeholders. Which word correctly completes this sentence?
A   Corporate governance
B   Social responsibility
C   Environmental

(1 mark)

45 The informal organisation arises out of which of the following?
A   Positions and/or responsibilities of employees
B   Personal or social relationships between employees
C   Organisational structure

(1 mark)

46 Which of the following is a source of external information?
A   Payroll system
B   Auditor's report
C   Annual budget
D   Marketing plan

(2 marks)

47 Which of the following is not a feature of good corporate governance?
A   Accountability towards shareholders
B   Less involvement of board
C   Ethical treatment to stakeholders
D   Transparency in financial information

(2 marks)

48 The practice of separation between ownership and control exists mainly for which type of organisations?
A   Large publicly limited companies
B   Small owner operated businesses
C   Professional partnership firms
D   Non government organisations

(2 marks)

49 Which of the following statements is correct?
  A   The direct service provision department provides services directly on a client's premises
  B   The marketing department ascertains the current and future needs of customers
  C   The finance department serves a purely support function

                                                                                         (1 mark)

50 An organisation which has high uncertainty avoidance is likely to adopt which of the following cultures?
  A   Power culture
  B   Role culture
  C   Task culture
  D   Person culture

                                                                                         (2 marks)

51 Committees are particularly effective at carrying out an organisation's routine marketing activities. Is this statement true or false?
  A   True
  B   False

                                                                                         (1 mark)

52 Unlike professions, occupations have a regulatory body. Is this statement true or false?
  A   True
  B   False

                                                                                         (1 mark)

QUESTION BANK

MIXED QUESTIONS

1 Which two of the following are the disadvantages of a scalar chain authority structure?

☐ It results in a rigid organisation

☐ Assignment of duties and responsibilities is unclear

☐ There is no coordination between management, supervisors and employees

☐ Time taken for suggestions to reach executives is too long

(2 marks)

2 Match the four cultural stereotypes with their principles. .

1 Encouragement for team approach
2 Shaped by rules, procedures and authority definitions
3 All authority rests with one individual
4 Strong values and beliefs on the "way things need to be done"

A Apollo organisation ☐

B Dionysus organisation ☐

C Athena organisation ☐

D Zeus organisation ☐

(2 marks)

3 Which of the following is an advantage of a manual accounting system over a computerised accounting system?

○ A manual system is less error prone

○ A manual system is less expensive to run over the long term

○ A manual system is cheaper and faster to implement

○ A manual system is easier to upgrade

(2 marks)

4 Which of the following best describes corporate social responsibility?

○ Only involves compliance with legislation

○ Contrary to the interests of shareholders

○ Increases cost of business activities

○ Can be viewed as investment

(2 marks)

(5) Match the information systems with their features.
1 Generates regular reports for the executives of the organisation
2 Records and processes routine transactions
3 Comprises a set of tools that allows the managers to run various "what if" scenarios
4 Performs traditional paper-based tasks electronically

A Decision support system ☐

B Office automation system ☐

C Management information system ☐

D Transaction processing system ☐

(2 marks)

6 State whether the following statements about stakeholder mapping are true or false?
(i) Stakeholders with a high level of power but low interest are most important
(ii) Stakeholders with low interest and power are of medium importance
(iii) The least important stakeholder groups are those with high interest and a high level of power

○ All are true
○ All are false
○ (i) and (iii) are true
○ (i) and (ii) are false

(2 marks)

7 Ethics refers to abiding by a set of written and unwritten rules based on both _____ and _____. Which set of words correctly completes this sentence/
○ (i) Compliance (ii) Suitability
○ (i) Lucidity (ii) Objectivity
○ (i) Socialism (ii) Professionalism
○ (i) Legality (ii) Morality

(2 marks)

8 The more minorities, ethnic groups and nationalities present in an organisation's workforce, the more concentrated its culture is likely to be. Is this statement true or false?
○ True
○ False

(1 mark)

9 An organisation has recently been accused of having pesticides in its products. What type of committee would it assemble to handle this problem?
○ Ad-hoc committee
○ Standing committee
○ Steering committee ?

(1 mark)

10 Lotus Smart Suite is an example of which of the following?
○ Office automation system
○ Transaction processing system
○ Management information system
○ Decision support system

(2 marks)

11

Executive

Manager —————————→ Secretary

Employee ←————— Employee ←————— Employee

Which type of communication is demonstrated by the diagram above?

○ Formal communication

○ Informal communication

(1 mark)

12 Information on which two of the following factors is required for strategic decision making?

☐ The external environment

☐ Macroeconomic factors and demographic patterns

☐ Performance of the organisation's workforce

☐ Past sales data

(2 marks)

13 Tom works at a multinational bank which has clear guidelines detailing the roles and responsibilities of all employees and each employee has a narrow span of control. Dick is working in an IT consultancy business where all employees are given a great deal of autonomy and each employee has a wide span of control. Match Tom and Dick with the type of organisation each is working for.

	Flat organisation	Tall organisation
Tom	○	○
Dick	○	○

(2 marks)

14 According to Hofstede, national cultures in which people are willing to accept innovative ideas and unconventional thoughts indicate which of the following?

○ High individualism

○ Low uncertainty avoidance

○ High long-term orientation

○ Low power distance

(2 marks)

15 Good corporate governance demands that non-executive directors be independent of the management and be free from any business dealings with the organisation. Is this statement true or false?

○ True

○ False

(1 mark)

16   Mendelow's stakeholder mapping matrix

INTEREST

	High	**Low**

		High	Low
POWER	**Low**	A	B
	High	D	C

Which category of stakeholders from the above matrix should an organisation 'keep informed' (A, B, C or D)?

○   **A**
○   **B**
○   **C**
○   **D**

(2 marks)

17   Which of the following statements are true in the context of the Anthony hierarchy?

A   Tactical decisions are taken at operational level
B   Managers decide where the organisation should strive to be in the future
C   Executives are involved in the day-to-day aspects of running the business

○   A and B
○   B and C
○   All of them
○   None of them

(2 marks)

18   Select the internal stakeholders of a limited company.
☐   Managers
☐   Owners
☐   Executive directors
☐   Employees
☐   Partners
☐   Non-executive directors
☐   Customers

(2 marks)

19 The following is the organisational chart of DishOne Ltd, a company that provides cable television services.

```
                    ┌──────────────┐
                    │  DishOne Ltd │
                    └──────┬───────┘
        ┌──────────┬───────┴────────┬─────────────┐
        ▼          ▼                ▼             ▼
  ┌───────────┐ ┌──────────┐ ┌─────────────┐ ┌──────────────┐
  │ Marketing │ │ Billing &│ │ After sales │ │ Installation │
  │           │ │ Enquiries│ │   service   │ │              │
  └───────────┘ └──────────┘ └─────────────┘ └──────────────┘
```

Which organisational structure does the above diagram represent?

○ Divisional
○ Functional
○ Departmental
○ Entrepreneurial

(2 marks)

20 In accordance with the best practices of effective corporate governance, which two of the following are the responsibilities of an audit committee?

☐ Reviewing the organisation's financial statements and internal control
☐ Determining appropriate remuneration packages for executives
☐ Appointing the external auditors and determining their remuneration
☐ Scrutinising the performance of the board of directors

(2 marks)

21 Which of the following statements about formal and informal organisations is correct?

(i) Informal organisation is based on employees' friendship and common interests
(ii) Informal organisation is always destructive and unreliable
(iii) The purpose of both the formal and informal organisation is to help organisation achieve its goals

○ (i) only
○ (i) and (ii)
○ (ii) and (iii)
○ (iii) only

(2 marks)

22 Which of the following are the functions of marketing in an organisation? Tick all those that apply.

☐ Creating value to customers
☐ Controlling organisation's money supply
☐ Delivering value to customers
☐ Communicating value to customers
☐ Ensuring overall day-to-day functioning of the organisation
☐ Managing customer relationships
☐ Market segmentation
☐ Market research

(2 marks)

23 Which two of the following are not the fundamental principles within the ACCA Code of Ethics and Conduct?

☐ Objectivity
☐ Integrity
☐ Transparency
☐ Confidentiality
☐ Professional behaviour
☐ Reliability

(2 marks)

24 Are the following established forms of organisational design?

	Yes	No
Entrepreneurial	O	O
Product	O	O

(2 marks)

25 Business organisations will contain only formal groups. Is this statement true or false?
- O True
- O False

(1 mark)

26 According to Charles Handy's four cultural stereotypes, which of the following organisations would adopt a role culture?
- O A large traditional corporate
- O An owner / operated enterprise
- O An NGO
- O A public sector organisation

(2 marks)

27 An audit committee is an example of what type of committee?
- O Ad-hoc committee
- O Standing committee
- O Project committee
- O Financial committee

(2 marks)

28 Loweita Ltd has an overseas factory in a country that allows child labour. The company states that because this practice is legal it can use child labour in its factory. Which of the following terms best describes Loweita's behaviour?
- O Ethical
- O Unethical
- O Illegal
- O Legal

(2 marks)

29 Ethics provide people with a clear cut direction to follow in terms of decision making. Is this statement true or false?
- O True
- O False

(1 mark)

30 A recent trend in corporate governance has been to increase the accountability of _____. Which word correctly completes this sentence?
- O Executive directors
- O Non executive directors
- O Managers
- O Shareholders

(2 marks)

QUESTION BANK

MULTIPLE CHOICE QUESTIONS

1   When an organisation analyses political, economic, social and technological factors, it is conducting what type of a scan?
    A   An environmental scan
    B   A marketing scan
    C   A strategic scan
    D   An operational scan

    (2 marks)

2   Which of the following is not one of the five forces that Porter identifies as affecting the competitiveness of an industry?
    A   Threat of new entrants
    B   Bargaining power of buyers
    C   Technological advances
    D   Threat of substitute products

    (2 marks)

3   Which of the following refers to fiscal policy?
    A   The regulation of financial intermediaries by the government
    B   The actions of the central bank in controlling the money supply
    C   The public spending and taxation policies set by the government
    D   The foreign trade and exchange rate policies of the government

    (2 marks)

4   Political systems and government policy cannot directly affect a business organisation. Is this statement true or false?
    A   True
    B   False

    (1 mark)

5   In which type of industry is an intense rivalry between competing organisations unlikely?
    A   When the competitors are in balance
    B   When the industry is a "sunrise" industry
    C   When the industry is a "sunset" or mature industry
    D   When there are high fixed costs in the industry

    (2 marks)

6   The "grey economy" prevalent in many countries today is caused by a(n) _____ birth rate and a(n) _____ death rate. Which of the following correctly completes the sentence?
    A   Increasing, increasing
    B   Decreasing, increasing
    C   Decreasing, decreasing
    D   Increasing, decreasing

    (2 marks)

7   Which of the following statements is incorrect with respect to The Data Protection Act?
    A   Both manual and computerised information must comply with the Act
    B   The law regulates how personal data is to be collected, stored, processed and used
    C   The Act attempts to protect individuals and corporate bodies that the data relates to
    D   The Act states the principles of data protection

    (2 marks)

8   Most individuals, households and businesses often benefit from the decrease in the level of business activity within an economy. Is this statement true or false?
    A   True
    B   False

    (1 mark)

9   The country Ruraltania imports $500 million worth of goods and services and also exports $275 million worth of goods and services. Which one of the following will Ruraltania have?
    A   A balance of payments deficit of $225
    B   A balance of payments surplus of $225
    C   A balance of payments equilibrium

(1 mark)

10 Which of the following statements is incorrect in the case of an economic environment of high price inflation?
    A   Those who owe money will gain and those who are owed money will lose
    B   It will result in a deficit in the balance of payments for a country
    C   The real income of individuals with fixed income will fall
    D   None of the above

(2 marks)

11 The more competitive the rivalry among existing firms in an industry, the higher the level of profits earned by the firms in that industry. Is this statement true or false?
    A   True
    B   False

(1 mark)

12 The term "stagflation" signifies the existence of which of the following?
    A   High unemployment and low inflation
    B   Low unemployment and high inflation
    C   Rising inflation and declining GDP
    D   Declining inflation and rising GDP

(2 marks)

13 Full employment, _____, economic growth and balance of payments equilibrium are the four main macro-economic policy objectives. Which word correctly completes the sentence?
    A   Increase in consumption
    B   Price stability
    C   Decrease in money supply
    D   Investment stability

(2 marks)

14 If an employee is found guilty of accessing information he is not entitled to see, the organisation does not have any grounds for rightful termination. Is this statement true or false?
    A   True
    B   False

(1 mark)

15 Economic growth for a country occurs when its _____ rises. Which word correctly completes this sentence?
    A   Gross National Product
    B   Net National Product
    C   Gross Domestic Product
    D   Net Domestic Product

(2 marks)

16 Which of the following statements about outsourcing is incorrect?
    (i)   Outsourcing refers to contracting a business process to an external organisation
    (ii)   Outsourcing leads to the loss of economies of scale
    (iii)   The function being outsourced is considered core to the business
    (iv)   Outsourcing gives an organisation access to wider skills and knowledge

    A   (i) and (iv)
    B   (ii) and (iii)
    C   None of the above
    D   Only (iii)

(2 marks)

17 Increases in the money supply will result in _____ in the consumption of goods in the short run and _____ in prices in the long run.
    A   Increase, increase
    B   Increase, decrease
    C   Decrease, increase
    D   Decrease, decrease

(2 marks)

18 During a period of high price deflation, individuals should immediately purchase goods and services they may need for the future. Is this statement true or false?
    A   True
    B   False

(1 mark)

19 A company has advertised for a position which only unmarried candidates can apply for. Which of the following is the legal term for this unlawful practice?
    A   Indirect discrimination
    B   Direct discrimination
    C   Implied discrimination
    D   Positive discrimination

(2 marks)

20 The increasing demand for environmentally-friendly hybrid cars is an example of which set of environmental factors?
    A   Social
    B   Technological
    C   Demographic
    D   Legal

(2 marks)

21 Which is one of the main methods governments use to control inflation?
    A   Raise interest rates
    B   Reduce public expenditure
    C   Increase taxes

(1 mark)

22 Savila Ltd has reduced a large number of its employees as a result of the automation of most of its operations. What is this known as?
    A   Lay-off
    B   Degrading
    C   Downsizing
    D   Delayering

(2 marks)

23 What is the meaning of GDP?
    A   The total manufacturing output in the economy
    B   The difference between total exports and total imports of a country
    C   The difference between public expenditure and public revenues
    D   The total production of goods and services in the economy

(2 marks)

24 "Trend" is a brand known for expensive luxury goods for people with a lavish lifestyle. A change in which of the following factors within a country will greatly impact the demand for Trend's products?
    A   Household patterns
    B   Age Groups
    C   Collective values of a society
    D   Social structure

(2 marks)

25 Delayering results in a bureaucratic and slow moving organisation. Is this statement true or false?
    A   True
    B   False

(1 mark)

26 Why is it important for organisations to maintain health and safety in the workplace?
    (i)   An organisation is liable to pay damages / compensation to the injured employee
    (ii)   It is a legal obligation for organisations
    (iii) An organisation has a responsibility to maintain a "duty of care" towards its employees

    A   (i) and (ii)
    B   (ii) and (iii)
    C   (i) and (iii)
    D   (i), (ii) and (ii)

(2 marks)

27   Which set of environmental factors would a trade union group try to influence?
    A   Economic
    B   Technological
    C   Demographic
    D   Political

(2 marks)

28   Governments often place import duties or quotas on foreign goods as a reaction against a balance of payments surplus. Is this statement true or false?
    A   True
    B   False

(1 mark)

29   Which of the following are the two types of jurisdictions or legal authorities that exist in most countries?
    A   Social and criminal
    B   Regional and national
    C   Local and international
    D   Political and legal

(2 marks)

30   Which of the following is an example of a supranational body?
    A   The United Nations
    B   The central bank of England
    C   The US Federal Reserve
    D   Amnesty International

(2 marks)

31   A UK IT consultancy firm is losing much of its business to Indian IT firms. What type of environment factor does this represent?
    A   Political
    B   Technological
    C   Social
    D   Economic

(2 marks)

32   The unemployment rate and inflation rate are inversely proportional. Is this statement true or false?
    A   True
    B   False

(1 mark)

33   Which of the following is not an example of a country's demographic factors?
    A   Population size
    B   Population growth rate
    C   Average income rate
    D   Education levels

(2 marks)

34   Delayering typically results in which type of organisational structure?
    A   Taller
    B   Wider
    C   Flatter
    D   Narrow

(2 marks)

35   Sam is interested in starting a real estate consultancy business. What is the main competitive factor of this particular industry?
    A   Threat of new entrants
    B   Bargaining power of buyers
    C   Bargaining power of suppliers
    D   High government intervention and regulation

(2 marks)

QUESTION BANK

MIXED QUESTIONS

1   Which of the following is the main purpose of the law in regard to the individual and employment? Tick all those which apply.

☐   Treating all employees equally
☐   Providing employees with adequate benefits
☐   Protecting employees from unfair termination
☐   Protecting employees from discrimination

(2 marks)

2   Which two of the following would be macro-economic policy objectives of a government?

☐   To achieve a balance between the country's imports and exports
☐   To ensure 100% employment
☐   To maximise economic growth
☐   To achieve stable prices

(2 marks)

3   The following are the effects of technological change on the organisational structure and strategy, except one. Which one is the exception?

○   Delayering
○   Outsourcing
○   Downgrading
○   Downsizing

(2 marks)

4   The unemployment rate in a country has recently risen from 6% to 9%. What will be the government's most likely response?

○   Raise interest rates by 3%
○   Increase public expenditure
○   Lower interest rates by 3%
○   Decrease public expenditure

(2 marks)

5   Are the following statements about the bargaining power of buyers true or false?

	True	False
It is high when the cost of switching to an alternative supplier is high	○	○
It is low when there is a concentration of buyers	○	○

(2 marks)

6   Changes in social trends can have a great impact on both business outcomes and the economy. Is this statement true or false?

○   False
○   True

(1 mark)

7 Which of the following is not a principle of data protection in relation to personal information?

○ Information should be obtained only for a specified and lawful purpose

○ Information should be relevant

○ Information should be accurate and up-to-date

○ Information should be maintained for at least ten years

(2 marks)

8 Under which two factors of a PESTEL analysis will "introduction of new taxes" and "changes in employment laws" be listed?

☐ Legal

☐ Economic

☐ Political

☐ Social

(2 marks)

9 Which of the following is the name given to unemployment arising from long-term changes in the conditions of an industry?

○ Structural unemployment

○ Cyclical unemployment

○ Frictional unemployment

○ Seasonal unemployment

(2 marks)

10 An airline has placed an advertisement for female flight attendants with three to five years of experience. Which of the following is the legal term for this unlawful practice?

○ Direct discrimination

○ Indirect discrimination

○ Implicit discrimination

○ Explicit discrimination

(2 marks)

11 Which two of the following statements about monetary policy are true?

☐ Monetary policy involves managing aggregate demand in the economy

☐ There is an inverse relationship between interest rate and level of public expenditure

☐ The key objective of monetary policy is to achieve price stability

(1 mark)

12 Which of the following tools can a government use to respond to increasing disparities in income and wealth between the different classes of a society?

○ Interest rates

○ Taxation rates

○ Exchange rates

○ Inflation rates

(2 marks)

13 Trikon Ltd has decided to move to a flatter and decentralised organisational structure. Which of the following strategies will Trikon adopt in order to implement its decision?

○ Downsizing

○ Outsourcing

○ Delayering

(1 mark)

14 Airline companies routinely offer discounts and promotional packages to their customers as a response to which one of the following competitive factors?

○ Bargaining power of customers

○ Threat of new entrants

○ Competitive rivalry

○ Threat of substitutes

(2 marks)

QUESTION BANK

SECTION C - HISTORY AND ROLE OF ACCOUNTING IN BUSINESS

MULTIPLE CHOICE QUESTIONS

1   Which one of the following is not a recommended qualitative characteristic that companies' accounting policies and financial statements should have?
A   Probability
B   Relevance
C   Reliability
D   Comparability

(2 marks)

2   A system of checks and controls is not required for automated business and financial systems. Is this statement true or false?
A   True
B   False

(1 mark)

3   What is the main role of the accounting department?
A   To maintain financial control
B   To track all the financial transactions of an organisation
C   To prepare budgets and maintain budgetary control
D   To provide accurate financial information to the users

(2 marks)

4   In which of these activities does the accounting department get involved with the production department?
(i)   Preparing the production budget
(ii)   Recording all the costs associated with production
(iii)   Determining the product price
(iv)   Accounting for all goods returned to a supplier

A   (i) and (ii)
B   (ii) and (iii)
C   (i) and (iv)
D   (iii) and (iv)

(2 marks)

5   Which one of the following is not a factor an organisation takes into consideration when deciding the credit level to be granted to a customer?
A   The reputation and financial stability of the companies the customer deals with
B   The importance of the customer to the organisation
C   The customer's payment history
D   The credit checks that have been obtained

(2 marks)

6   Failure to maintain proper accounting records is a criminal offence. Is this statement true or false?
A   True
B   False

(1 mark)

7   In 1494 an Italian mathematician, Luca Pacioli, introduced the _____. Which word correctly completes this sentence?
A   Double entry book-keeping system
B   Geometrical tools
C   Concept of stewardship

(1 mark)

8   Zukin Ltd finds it difficult to make payments to its suppliers and employees on time because of a cash shortage due to the credit terms granted to its customers. Which of Zukin's financial systems is working inefficiently?

    A   Payroll
    B   Credit control
    C   Purchases and sales invoicing
    D   Working capital management

(2 marks)

9   Which of following is the main objective of the International Accounting Standards Board (IASB)?

    A   Creating laws on accounting
    B   Monitoring compliance with accounting standards
    C   Ensuring that all countries follow the same accounting methods
    D   Developing a single set of global accounting standards

(2 marks)

10   Which of the following statements about accounting information is incorrect?

    A   It is financial information about economic activities
    B   It provides information about future events
    C   It provides the basis for making decisions about resource allocation
    D   It can be used to monitor how a business actually performs in comparison with the estimates

(2 marks)

11   _____is an example of a spreadsheet application. Which word correctly completes this sentence?

    A   MS Access
    B   Oracle
    C   MS Excel
    D   MySQL

(2 marks)

12   Which of the following is not a function of the accounting department?

    A   Cash management
    B   Budgeting
    C   Treasury
    D   Variance analysis

(2 marks)

13   Which of the following requirements must a company fulfil in order to be listed on a stock exchange?

    A   Have a minimum level of profitability
    B   Have a minimum number of shareholders
    C   Maintain and report detailed financial information
    D   Report and pay a high level of taxes

(2 marks)

14   Which of the following is an aim of the financial control system relating to sales?

    (i)   To ensure that orders are processed and fulfilled
    (ii)   To ensure that all the credits are duly paid
    (iii)   To meet the monthly sales targets set by the top management
    (iv)   To track and monitor the payment status of each order

    A   (iii) and (iv)
    B   (ii) and (iii)
    C   (i) and (iv)
    D   (i) and (ii)

(2 marks)

15   Which of the following is an advantage of a manual financial system over a computerised financial system?

    A   Accurate and reliable
    B   Increased effort of accountants
    C   Less expensive and easy to secure
    D   Easy back up and restoration of records

(2 marks)

QUESTION BANK

MIXED QUESTIONS

1 Which two of the following are not features of a database system application?
☐ Allows users to run various "what if" scenarios
☐ Allows users to run "queries"
☐ Allows users to retrieve specific sets of data
☐ Allows users to use shortcuts when performing mathematical calculations

(2 marks)

2 Along with the financial condition of the organisation, which the other two financial details does the annual return statement include?
☐ Share price
☐ Tax liability
☐ Level of profits

(1 mark)

3 Which of the following aspects of a marketing function would the accounting department be involved with?
(i) Developing a marketing strategy
(ii) Preparing sales and marketing budget
(iii) Determining the product price
(iv) Deciding the payment terms with outside vendors

○ (i) and (iii)
○ (ii), (iii) and (iv)
○ (ii) and (iii)
○ (i), (ii) and (iii)

(2 marks)

4 Which two of the following are control features of a purchasing system?
☐ All the orders for purchases are properly authorised
☐ Orders are placed with suppliers quoting the lowest price
☐ All the purchases are recorded accurately
☐ All received purchases are accepted and paid for

(2 marks)

5 Which of the following is not an input of a payroll system?
○ Payslip
○ Attendance sheet
○ Details of salary deductions

(1 mark)

6 Are the following statements about computerised financial system true or false?

	True	False
It is faster to develop than the manual financial system	○	○
It secures data better than the manual financial system	○	○

(2 marks)

QUESTION BANK

SECTION D - SPECIFIC FUNCTIONS OF ACCOUNTING AND INTERNAL FINANCIAL CONTROL

MULTIPLE CHOICE QUESTIONS

1   John is mainly involved in the interest and currency exchange rate management of a large multinational corporation. Which of the following business functions is John a part of?
    A   Treasury
    B   Finance
    C   Accounts
    D   Costing
                                                                                                    (2 marks)

2   The internal auditor would be responsible for implementing the internal control system of an organisation. Is this statement true or false?
    A   True
    B   False
                                                                                                    (1 mark)

3   Which of the following is not a function of an external auditor?
    (i)   Detecting fraud and errors
    (ii)   Adding value and improving client's operations
    (iii)   Reviewing client's internal control system
    (iv)   Reporting on client's financial performance to its shareholders

    A   (i) and (iii)
    B   (ii) and (iv)
    C   (ii) and (iii)
    B   (i) and (iv)
                                                                                                    (2 marks)

4   Which of the following should not be included in the job description of an internal auditor?
    A   Evaluating the internal control systems
    B   Reviewing the safeguarding of assets
    C   Reporting on whether the financial statements are free of material misstatements
    D   Reviewing the risk management practices
                                                                                                    (2 marks)

5   Working capital management involves managing the _____ to finance the _____ of an organisation. Which set of words correctly completes this sentence?
    A   (i) Long-term borrowings   (ii) Capital investments
    B   (i) Short-term assets and liabilities (ii) Operating requirements
    C   (i) Cash flow   (ii) Interest payments
    D   (i) Share capital   (ii) Production costs
                                                                                                    (2 marks)

6   The implementation of a system of checks and balances is the responsibility of the external auditor. Is this statement true or false?
    A   True
    B   False
                                                                                                    (1 mark)

7   The UK government has just announced that any profits made on investments by organisations will be tax-free. This will have the greatest impact on which department of an organisation?

  A Accounting
  B Manufacturing
  C Treasury
  D Marketing

    (2 marks)

8   The controls associated with an internal control system can be classified as _____. Which set of words correctly completes this sentence?

  A Managerial controls and executive controls
  B Administrative controls and accounting controls
  C General controls and specific controls
  D Production controls and non-production controls

    (2 marks)

9   Which of the following situations indicate the occurrence of fraud?

  (i) The collection officer receives payment of $120 from a customer; he deposits $240 with the cashier
  (ii) An employee spends $550 of his own money for official purposes and submits bills of $530 for reimbursement of his expenses
  (iii) The purchase invoice received from a supplier is of $890; the purchase officer records the payment due to the supplier as $980
  (iv) The amount received from a customer for goods sold is $3,500; the sales officer raises a sales invoice for $2,800 and records $700 as discount allowed

  A (i) and (iii)
  B (i), (ii) and (iv)
  C (iii) and (iv)
  D Only (iii)

    (2 marks)

10   Sandol Ltd offers a wide range of home and personal care products. The marketing manager of Sandol will take decisions about its product mix (set or combination of products offered for sale) with the help of _____. Which word correctly completes this sentence?

  A Management accountant
  B Financial accountant
  C Finance manager

    (1 mark)

11   Which of the following best describes fraud in the business context?

  A Avoiding an obligation with the intention of obtaining an advantage
  B Complicated financial transactions conducted by 'white collar' criminals
  C Forging of securities and monetary instruments
  D Intentional misrepresentation of the financial position of the business

    (2 marks)

12   What is the reasonable assurance that an external auditor will primarily seek from the system of internal control?

  A The cost of internal control doesn't exceed its benefits
  B Operational efficiency has been achieved
  C Errors have been prevented or detected
  D Management cannot override the system

    (2 marks)

13   Which of the following situations refers to the concept of "teeming and lading"?

  A A sales payment from one customer is misappropriated
  B A payment that has to be made to an organisation's supplier is overstated
  C A cash payment received from a customer is understated
  D An organisation's assets are used by employees for personal purposes

    (2 marks)

14   One of the main objectives of a system of internal checks is detecting fraud and errors. Is this statement true or false?

    A   True

    B   False

                      (1 mark)

15   Which of the following is concerned with testing and evaluating internal controls within an organisation?

    A   Operational audit

    B   Systems audit

    C   Transaction audit

    D   Social responsibility audit

                      (2 marks)

16   Management accounting is primarily concerned with providing information to _____. Which of the following correctly completes this sentence?

    A   External users

    B   Internal users

    C   Both internal and external users

                      (1 mark)

17   To whom is the external auditor primarily accountable?

    A   The government

    B   The board of directors

    C   The audit committee

    D   The shareholders

                      (2 marks)

18   Which one of the following data security techniques is most appropriate for protecting data while it is being transmitted?

    A   Restricted access

    B   Encryption

    C   Check sums

                      (1 mark)

19   Which of the following is not a consequence of fraud for an organisation?

    A   Difficulties in borrowing funds from outside

    B   Unfair and untrue financial statements

    C   Loss of credibility

    D   Whistle-blowing

                      (2 marks)

20   In the context of methods of controlling IT systems and software, the use of locks and a card entry system are examples of which of the following?

    A   Biometric control

    B   Network access control

    C   Input control

    D   Physical access control

                      (2 marks)

21   Designing an effective internal control system reduces the possibility of fraud in an organisation. Is this statement true or false?

    A   True

    B   False

                      (1 mark)

22   What is the role of the finance function within an organisation?

    (i)   Monitoring working capital usage

    (ii)   Researching and selecting sources of funding

    (iii)   Budgeting and budgetary control

    (iv)   Reporting on the organisation's state of affairs

    A   (i) and (ii)

    B   (ii) and (iv)

    C   (i), (ii) and (iii)

    D   All of the above

                      (2 marks)

23 Which is the financial statement that shows the revenues earned and expenses incurred of the organisation for a particular period?

    A   Statement of financial position

    B   Statement of comprehensive income

    C   Statement of cash flows

    D   Statement of retained earnings

(2 marks)

24 The control that is designed to prevent, detect and correct errors in transactions as they flow through the various stages of a specific business or data processing system is called _____. Which word correctly completes this sentence?

    A   An application control

    B   A specific control

    C   A general control

    D   A system control

(2 marks)

25 Monitoring of the business environment would help management to prevent and detect fraud. Is this statement true or false?

    A   True

    B   False

(1 mark)

26 In which of the following departments is fraud most likely to arise?

    A   Human resources

    B   Production

    C   Sales

    D   Marketing

(2 marks)

27 Internal control is designed to provide reasonable assurance regarding the achievement of objectives in the following categories except one. Which is the exception?

    A   Reliability of financial reporting

    B   Compliance with applicable laws and regulations

    C   Adherence to core values and mission

    D   Operational effectiveness and efficiency

(2 marks)

28 A production department of a company needs a CNC machine for a period of 5 years. The production manager needs to decide whether to buy the machine or rent it from a vendor for 5 years. Who can help the production manager in this decision?

    A   The financial controller

    B   The finance manager

    C   The management accountant

    D   The treasurer

(2 marks)

29 Which one of the following is not one of the terms that can be used to describe the accounting process?

    A   Publication

    B   Presentation

    C   Recognition

    D   Measurement

(2 marks)

30 Mitigating business tax liabilities is an illegal activity. Is this statement true or false?

    A   True

    B   False

(1 mark)

31 Which test does an auditor use to discover errors and omissions in financial accounts?

    A   Substantive test

    B   Compliance test

(1 mark)

32 Which of the following statements about internal and external auditors is incorrect?
  A   Internal and external auditors may coordinate to minimise duplication of work
  B   Both internal and external auditors need to be independent, if they are to be effective
  C   Internal auditor is appointed by the board of directors and external auditor is appointed by the shareholders
  D   The procedures used by internal and external auditors are very different

                                                                                                      (2 marks)

33 Safeguarding of assets is an example of which type of control?
  A   Accounting control
  B   Administrative control
  C   Production control
  D   Financial control

                                                                                                      (2 marks)

34 System recovery procedures are an example of which type of control of an IT system?
  A   Failure control
  B   Processing control
  C   Security control
  D   Output control

                                                                                                      (2 marks)

35 The management deliberately shows an improvement in the financial performance of a company by using deceptive accounting methods. Which of the following is a potential consequence of this type of fraud?
  A   Decrease in working capital
  B   Failure to provide the expected returns to investors
  C   Fall in dividend to shareholders
  D   Decrease in share price

                                                                                                      (2 marks)

36 An organisation's inventory count at the year-end showed a lower value than in the books of accounts. It was discovered that some inventory items had been stolen by an employee. This indicates failure of the _____controls of the organisation. Which word correctly completes this sentence?
  A   General
  B   Administrative
  C   Non-financial
  D   Accounting

                                                                                                      (2 marks)

MIXED QUESTIONS

1

1   The actual value of stock at the stores is $9,000 but the accountant overvalues it at $10,000
2   The salesman uses the sample of goods provided to him for demonstration purposes for his personal use
3   The purchase clerk records an amount due to a supplier as $1,000 whereas the actual amount due is $950

Match the following with the above mentioned situations.

A   Cash fraud   ☐

B   Asset fraud   ☐

C   Manipulation of financial statements   ☐

(2 marks)

2   Which of the following are security measures to stop unauthorised access to data / computer system / private information? Tick all those which apply.
☐   Password
☐   Firewall
☐   Network access control
☐   Audit trail

(2 marks)

3   Which two of the following statements about external auditors are correct?
☐   External auditors are required by law to be professionally qualified accountants
☐   External auditors are appointed by management
☐   External auditors are mainly concerned with reviewing internal control systems and procedures
☐   External auditors report to the shareholders of a company

(2 marks)

4   The external auditor selects some transactions in each functional area and checks them paying special attention to evidence about whether or not the control features are in operation. This is an example of which of the following?
○   Operational test
○   Substantive test
○   Control test
○   Compliance test

(2 marks)

5   Match the following functions (A, B, C and D) with the relevant activities (1, 2, 3 and 4).

A	Financial accounting	1	Evaluating the most suitable source for borrowing funds
B	Management accounting	2	Placing organisation's funds into viable investment options
C	Finance	3	Identifying, recording, classifying and analysing costs
D	Treasury	4	Codifying and processing financial information

A   ☐

B   ☐

C   ☐

D   ☐

(2 marks)

6   Who are involved in and responsible for the prevention and the detection of fraud in an organisation? Tick all those which apply.
☐   Accountants
☐   Managers
☐   Internal auditor
☐   Board of directors

(2 marks)

7   Can the following activities be classified as an "event" in accounting terminology while recording financial information?

	Yes	No
An organisation's inventory is damaged as a result of flooding	○	○
An organisation purchases a fleet of new vehicles	○	○

(2 marks)

8   Which two of the following are management accounting functions within the organisation?
☐   Working capital management and risk assessment
☐   Purchase ledger, sales invoicing and payroll
☐   Inventory valuation and reporting
☐   Budgeting, budgetary control and variance analysis

(2 marks)

9   Are the following statements about internal auditors true or false?

	True	False
Internal auditors are always employees of an organisation.	○	○
Internal auditors report to the shareholders.	○	○

(2 marks)

10   According to the internal check of "segregation of duties", which of the following tasks shouldn't be performed by one person?
○   Receiving, checking and custody
○   Authorising, recording and custody
○   Executing, receiving payment and recording
○   Authorising, approving and executing

(2 marks)

11   Which of the following are features of an effective internal financial control procedure? Tick all those which apply.

☐   Management override

☐   A system of adequate internal checks

☐   Collusion among employees

☐   Explicit directives on the roles and responsibility of employees

(2 marks)

12   Which of the following increases the possibility of fraud for a multinational company?

○   Segregation of duties

○   Training and fraud awareness education

○   Performance-based reward system for managers

○   Implementation of a system of internal control

(2 marks)

QUESTION BANK

MULTIPLE CHOICE QUESTIONS

1   According to Fiedler's contingency model of leadership, leaders with which of the following traits will be effective in a tall organisation?
    A   Financial motivation
    B   Psychological motivation
    C   Task motivation
    D   Personal motivation

                                                                                    (2 marks)

2   Susan is dynamic and is driven to overcome obstacles. She focuses on her task and is committed to the team achieving its objectives. According to Belbin's theory, which role does Susan play in the team?
    A   Implementer
    B   Resource investigator
    C   Plant
    D   Shaper

                                                                                    (2 marks)

3   In his "management by objectives" theory, Drucker states that each employee should be given a set of SMART objectives. What does the M in SMART stand for?
    A   Manageable
    B   Motivational
    C   Measurable

                                                                                    (1 mark)

4   In Maslow's "hierarchy of needs" which is the highest or top level need of an individual?
    A   Self-actualisation
    D   Esteem
    C   Belonging
    D   Safety

                                                                                    (2 marks)

5   Which of the following is the correct order of stages in Tuckman's team development theory?
    A   Norming, performing, storming, adjourning, forming
    B   Adjourning, storming, norming, forming, performing
    C   Forming, storming, norming, performing, adjourning
    D   Performing, norming, storming, forming, adjourning

                                                                                    (2 marks)

6   According to the Ashridge model, the autocratic style of leader gives most autonomy and decision making powers to subordinates. Is this statement true or false?
    A   True
    B   False

                                                                                    (1 mark)

7   Jim gets along well with his colleagues and fits into the culture of the organisation. Which of his individual traits characterise his behaviour?
    A   Conscientiousness
    B   Attitudes
    C   Agreeableness
    D   Understanding

                                                                                    (2 marks)

8 Which of the following theories states that a manager has to be responsible for every aspect of his subordinate's job?

A   The classical theory of management

B   The scientific theory of management

C   The human relations school of management

D   The empirical school of management

(2 marks)

9 Which of the following statements is made by Taylor, the "father of scientific management"?

A   Management should organise large groups of employees into the overall structure of the organisation to increase the efficiency and output of each group

B   Workers should be remunerated on a "piece rate pay system" to increase their productivity

C   Individuals want more than just a paycheck from the organisation they work for and they perform better when empowered

D   Management should set a set of objectives for each employee and his performance should be measured against these objectives

(2 marks)

10 A team of IT professionals and finance domain experts put together to develop new software for a bank is which type of team?

A   Action team

B   Project team

C   Advisory team

(1 mark)

11 In which two categories did Herzberg classify the factors that lead to people's satisfaction or dissatisfaction within their work?

A   Intrinsic and extrinsic rewards

B   Valence and expectancy

C   Motivators and hygiene factors

D   Incentives and rewards

(2 marks)

12 According to Fiedler's theory, which are the three main factors which decide how favourable a situation is to a particular leader?

A   Leader position power, task structure, leader member relation

B   Leader member relation, team member relation, organisation structure

C   Task structure, organisation structure, leader position power

D   Leadership skills, leader member relation, leader position authority

(2 marks)

13 The main purpose of a team is to provide the necessary structure or framework and help team members meet their psychological needs. Is this statement true or false?

A   True

B   False

(1 mark)

14 Which of the following represents the first set of needs that people need to fulfil according to Maslow's hierarchy of needs?

A   Physiological

B   Love / belonging

C   Psychological

D   Self-actualisation

(2 marks)

15 What is the main difference between a group and a team?

A   Groups arrive at decisions by consensus whereas teams use a majority vote system

B   Groups in contrast to teams consist only of members that share similar characteristics

C   Groups only share a common purpose whereas teams have a specific goal to achieve

D   Groups are put together for a social purpose whereas teams are assembled for work

(2 marks)

16 Fred is a manager who is very involved with the day-to-day operations of his department i.e. he is very 'hands-on'. According to P. Drucker he has fallen into the _____ trap. Which word correctly completes this sentence?

    A   Operations

    B   Activity

    C   Detail

                                                                        (1 mark)

17 Which of the below four factors is least likely to influence the behaviour of a group?

    A   Composition of the group

    B   Size of the group

    C   Location of the group

    D   Group norms

                                                                        (2 marks)

18 Tom is a member of a production team in his organisation. He is very diplomatic and cooperative. He listens to other team members and avoids friction. Which of Belbin's team roles does Tom play in his team?

    A   Team worker

    B   Coordinator

    C   Shaper

    D   Implementer

                                                                        (2 marks)

19 The more cohesive a group is, the more likely it is to function efficiently. Is this statement true or false?

    A   True

    B   False

                                                                        (1 mark)

20 Star Ltd sent out a questionnaire based on Blake and Mounton's managerial grid to all its functional managers. The results of the questionnaire showed that Jennet demonstrates a 9.9 leadership style. Which of the following best describes Jennet's management style?

    A   Total concentration on getting the job done

    B   High work accomplishment from committed staff

    C   Thoughtful attention to staff needs

    D   Balancing the necessity to get work done with staff morale

                                                                        (2 marks)

21 The stage where a team starts settling down and the team members agree on work sharing and their roles is labelled by Tuckman as the _____ stage. Which word correctly completes this sentence?

    A   Forming

    B   Storming

    C   Norming

    D   Performing

                                                                        (2 marks)

22 Jim is consultative and believes that his subordinates can assume self-direction and control without the need for the threat of punishment. Which style of management does Jim adopt according to McGregor's theory?

    A   Theory X

    B   Theory Y

                                                                        (1 mark)

23 Neville is a very creative and imaginative individual. He has the ability to solve difficult problems but ignores details. Which one of Belbin's team roles is played by Neville?

    A   Monitor-Evaluator

    B   Resource investigator

    C   Implementer

    D   Plant

                                                                        (2 marks)

24   Which of the following terms does Bennis use to describe the ability of leaders to communicate effectively?
- **A**   Management of trust
- **B**   Management of self
- **C**   Management of attention
- **D**   Management of meaning

           (2 marks)

25   What are the three people-oriented roles identified by Belbin?
- **A**   Shaper, implementer, coordinator
- **B**   Plant, specialist, team worker
- **C**   Completer finisher, monitor evaluator, plant
- **D**   Coordinator, resource investigator, team worker

           (2 marks)

26   For a collection of people to be labelled as a team which of the following conditions must be satisfied?
- **A**   Members share a specific performance goal
- **B**   Members have similar characteristics
- **C**   Members share common interests
- **D**   Members have specific job category

           (2 marks)

27   Which of the following statements about leadership, management and supervision is true?
- (i)   Supervision involves setting a clear direction for people to follow
- (ii)   Management involves planning, organising, monitoring and controlling
- (iii)   Leadership requires the highest level of involvement and interaction with people
- (iv)   Leadership occurs through factors other than just formal authority

- **A**   (ii) and (iv)
- **B**   (i), (ii) and (iv)
- **C**   Only (ii)
- **D**   All of the above

           (2 marks)

28   Sam works as a software engineer in an IT company. He is always willing to take on additional responsibilities and new challenges to accomplish his own and his team's goals. What type of motivation exists for Sam as identified by D. McClelland?
- **A**   Affiliation motivation
- **B**   Power motivation
- **C**   Achievement motivation

           (1 mark)

29   Which of the following are the three broad categories of roles managers need to play according to Mintzberg?
- **A**   Educational, professional and interpersonal
- **B**   Interpersonal, informational and decision making
- **C**   Personal, promotional and informational
- **D**   Motivational, personal and decision making

           (2 marks)

30   Which of the following is not one of the factors that contribute to making a team effective?
- **A**   Team rewards
- **B**   Subordinate goals
- **C**   Skills and role clarity
- **D**   Supportive environment

           (2 marks)

31   The main areas of managerial responsibility are organising, leading and controlling. What word, describing the most important responsibility of managers, is missing from this sentence?
- **A**   Supervising
- **B**   Coordinating
- **C**   Planning
- **D**   Staffing

           (2 marks)

32   Henry is a manager who involves his subordinates in the decision making process and empowers them to make decisions on their own. Which school of thought / theory does Henry belong to?

    A   Scientific theory of management

    B   Classical theory of management

    C   Human relations school

    D   Management by objectives

                                                 (2 marks)

33   Which of the following collections of people constitute a group?

    A   A crowd waiting for a train

    B   Eight employees of an organisation who work for the same department

    C   All members of a particular voting district

    D   Forty people watching a movie in a cinema hall

                                                 (2 marks)

34   According to Herzberg's two-factor theory, the salary an employee receives is an example of which of the following?

    A   Motivator

    B   Hygiene factor

    C   Motivator and a Hygiene factor

                                                 (1 mark)

QUESTION BANK

MIXED QUESTIONS

1   Which of the following are hygiene factors according to Herzberg?

☐   Work conditions
☐   Salary
☐   Responsibilities
☐   Career progression
☐   Relationship with boss
☐   Growth
☐   Recognition
☐   Company policy

(2 marks)

2   Stuart is a highly realistic and disciplined individual. He always focuses on the practicality of any ideas or suggestions that are put forward. Which one of Belbin's team roles does Stuart fulfil?

○   Coordinator
○   Specialist
○   Implementer
○   Plant

(2 marks)

3   Match the managerial roles identified by Mintzberg with their role categories.

1   Disseminator
2   Figurehead
3   Negotiator

A   Decisional   ☐

B   Informational   ☐

C   Interpersonal   ☐

(2 marks)

4   For a collection of people to be defined as a group they must satisfy which two of the following conditions?

☐   Share many similar characteristics
☐   Interact with each other
☐   Influence each other
☐   Share similar work styles

(2 marks)

5 Jason leads a team of six experienced R&D scientists. They are currently executing their tasks as an organised unit. There is no intervention in the team's work from Jason. Which one of Tuckman's group stages is Jason's team at?

○ Norming

○ Forming

○ Storming

○ Performing

(2 marks)

6 According to Adair which three needs do effective leaders need to address?

☐ Organisational needs

☐ Functional needs

☐ Group needs

☐ Individual needs

☐ Task needs

☐ Strategic needs

(2 marks)

7 Which of the following benefits can be obtained by effective and correct use of teams?

(i) Enhanced performance

(ii) Development of social relationships

(iii) Fast consensus on decisions

(iv) Coordination and cooperation

○ (i) and (iii)

○ (ii) and (iv)

○ (i) and (iv)

○ (i), (iii) and (iv)

(2 marks)

8 Blake and Mouton's "country club" managers are those who have_____.
Select the two options that correctly complete this sentence.

☐ A high concern for people

☐ A low concern for people

☐ A high concern for production

☐ A low concern for production

(2 marks)

9 Playful Ltd has formed a squash club for its employees. The members of the club play squash against each other every Saturday. This club is an example of which of the following?

○ Formal group

○ Informal group

○ Official group

(1 mark)

10 Ted is the production manager of an organisation. He has studied the jobs of all his subordinates and developed a standardised way of doing each one. Which theory of management is he implementing?

○ Scientific theory of management

○ Classical theory of management

○ The human relations school

(1 mark)

11   Which of the following is not one of Fayol's 14 principles of management?
- ○   Division of authority
- ○   Unity of command
- ○   Esprit de corps
- ○   Discipline

(2 marks)

12   Which of the following are the three main categories of team roles identified by Belbin?
- ☐   Action
- ☐   Task
- ☐   People
- ☐   Decision
- ☐   Control
- ☐   Cerebral

(2 marks)

13   Which of the following are cerebral-oriented team roles according to Belbin's team roles theory?
- ☐   Implementer
- ☐   Completer
- ☐   Monitor Evaluator
- ☐   Resource Investigator
- ☐   Plant
- ☐   Shaper
- ☐   Specialist

(2 marks)

14   Match the following needs with appropriate categories based on Maslow's hierarchy of needs.
1   Status and recognition
2   Family and friendship
3   Morality and creativity
4   Food and shelter

A   Belonging needs   ☐

B   Self-actualisation needs   ☐

C   Physiological needs   ☐

D   Esteem needs   ☐

(2 marks)

15   Which of the following is not one of the three main components of Vroom's formula on motivation?
- ○   Valence
- ○   Expectancy
- ○   Instrumentality
- ○   Materiality

(2 marks)

16 Which of the following are not characteristics of effective teams? Tick all those which apply.

☐ Clarity on roles of individual members

☐ High interpersonal conflicts

☐ Reactive problem solving approach

☐ High commitment to team's targets

(2 marks)

17 James adopts an authoritarian style of management as he believes his subordinates dislike work and responsibilities and will avoid doing any if they can. According to McGregor, James is a theory _____ style of manager. Which word correctly completes this sentence?

○ Z

○ Y

○ X

○ W

(2 marks)

18 Which two of the following are intrinsic rewards?

☐ Non-cash incentives

☐ High morale

☐ Job satisfaction

☐ Fringe benefit

(2 marks)

QUESTION BANK

MULTIPLE CHOICE QUESTIONS

1   Terence has just joined a multinational bank as a management trainee. He has been assigned to Robert, a senior manager at the bank. Robert's role is to guide and advise Terence on aspects of his career. Robert is Terence's _____. Which word correctly completes this sentence?

    A   Coach

    B   Buddy

    C   Counsellor

    D   Mentor

(2 marks)

2   The simple communication model consists of sender, message, receiver, feedback and _____. Which word correctly completes this sentence?

    A   Static

    B   Noise

    C   Content

    D   Interruption

(2 marks)

3   Honey and Mumford describe people whose learning style involves understanding basic principles as _____. Which word correctly completes this sentence?

    A   Activists

    B   Theorists

    C   Pragmatists

    D   Reflectors

(2 marks)

4   The activity in which an organisation provides its employees with an opportunity to talk to another individual about personal problems they are facing is termed _____. Which word correctly completes this sentence?

    A   Mentoring

    B   Coaching

    C   Counselling

(1 mark)

5   Which of the following tests is used to measure certain qualities in candidates, such as their introversion, emotional stability and motivation?

    A   Intelligence tests

    B   Personality tests

    C   Competence tests

    D   Aptitude tests

(2 marks)

6   Which pattern of communication is the most efficient way to send a message?

    A   The circle

    B   The chain

    C   The Y

    D   The wheel

(2 marks)

7 Which of the following statements about the disadvantages of an interview is incorrect?
- **A** An interview can be ineffective if the interviewer is biased
- **B** Interviews are very objective in nature
- **C** An interviewee's behaviour often depends on the interviewer's behaviour

(1 mark)

8 The manager informs his team members that employees who complete all their work on a particular day can leave early. One of the team members thinks this means that everyone can leave early. Which of the following has caused this ineffective communication?
- **A** Use of ineffective language by the sender
- **B** Lost or distorted content
- **C** Preconceived notions of the receiver
- **D** Selective interpretation

(2 marks)

9 Edward is completing a performance appraisal of his subordinate, Arnold. He is very pleased with Arnold's interpersonal skills and bases the overall rating on this aspect of Arnold's performance. This is a barrier to effective appraisal and is known as _____. Which word correctly completes this sentence?
- **A** The isolation effect
- **B** The halo effect
- **C** The cluster effect
- **D** The job effect

(2 marks)

10 An informal communication system establishes how, where and why employees can and should communicate with each other. Is this statement true or false?
- **A** True
- **B** False

(1 mark)

11 Which one of the following is the best suited medium for an advertisement by a local courier company advertising a job vacancy for a mail-delivery person?
- **A** Local newspaper
- **B** Professional magazine
- **C** Recruitment agency
- **D** National newspaper

(2 marks)

12 A bank has a policy of involving an employee from its retail division and an employee from its commercial division whilst making joint marketing calls. This is an example of what kind of system?
- **A** Buddy
- **B** Coaching
- **C** Counselling
- **D** Mentoring

(2 marks)

13 Jerry has decided to enrol in computer training classes after work so as to better his career prospects. His decision is an example of which of the following?
- **A** Development
- **B** Training
- **C** Education

(1 mark)

14 Samantha has undertaken the performance appraisal of her subordinate, Harry. During the feedback stage she encouraged Harry to think of new ideas that will help him to improve his performance and she also provided some suggestions for improvement. Which approach of feedback is used by Samantha?
- **A** The tell and sell approach
- **B** The tell and listen approach
- **C** The problem solving approach
- **D** The 360 degree approach

(2 marks)

15 Which of the following is the second step in the training and development process?
  A   Programme design
  B   Delivery and validation
  C   Setting objectives
  D   Identifying needs

(2 marks)

16 A policy which states that no job applicant or employee should be treated unfairly because of factors such as race, religion or gender is referred as a(n) _____. Which word correctly completes this sentence?
  A   Diversity policy
  B   Equal opportunities policy
  C   Equal employment policy
  D   Diversification policy

(2 marks)

17 Effective performance appraisals help to evaluate the recruitment and selection process of an organisation. Is this statement true or false?
  A   True
  B   False

(1 mark)

18 John is the CEO of a multinational company. Mary is the CFO of a subsidiary of that company. Sara is the financial manager of the subsidiary. Sara informs Mary that the subsidiary's profits are reducing, and Mary tells John about this. Which pattern of communication has taken place between the three?
  A   The Circle
  B   The Chain
  C   The Wheel
  D   The Y

(2 marks)

19 Which of the following is the last stage of a personal development plan (PDP)?
  A   Routinely accessing the progress against the objectives set
  B   Examining the needs to amend existing PDP or create a new PDP
  C   Identifying an area for development and deciding the objectives
  D   Implementing the PDP

(2 marks)

20 The CEO of an organisation has just made a video in which he outlines what the company's long-term strategy and objectives will be. All employees must watch this video. This is an example of which type of communication?
  A   Downward communication
  B   Upward communication
  C   Lateral communication

(1 mark)

21 Which of the following statements about training, development and education is true?
  (i)   Training is a long-term process of self improvement
  (ii)   Education gives participants a specific skill set or knowledge base
  (iii) Training, development and education are all linked to and involve learning
  (iv)   Development is a lifelong process and comes from a number of sources

  A   (iv) only
  B   (ii) and (iii)
  C   (iii) only
  D   (i) and (ii)

(2 marks)

22 In most contemporary organisations, recruitment and selection responsibilities are handled independently by an HR department. Is this statement true or false?
  A   True
  B   False

(1 mark)

23 Which of the following steps is undertaken at each stage of a training and development process?
  A Validation
  B Identification of needs
  C Feedback and interaction
  D Setting of objectives

(2 marks)

24 Which of the following is not one of the ways of improving time management?
  A Making a "to-do" list that prioritises tasks
  B Setting a strict time limit for each meeting
  C Procrastinating
  D Taking calls only during a certain time

(2 marks)

25 The finance manager sending an e-mail to the HR manager to request employees' attendance records is which type of communication?
  A Spontaneous informal communication
  B Lateral formal communication
  C Unofficial upward communication
  D Formal downward communication

(2 marks)

26 All except one of the following are the attributes of effective communication. Which is the exception?
  A Clear
  B Correct
  C Concise
  D Creative

(2 marks)

27 Which of the following represents the tendency of a reviewer to give all members of a team the same rating during their performance appraisal regardless of their individual performances?
  A The contrast effect
  B The halo effect
  C The cluster effect
  D The isolation effect

(2 marks)

28 Tony enrols on a two-year part-time personnel management course so that he can move from the position of HR officer to HR manager. This is an example of which of the following?
  A Development
  B Training
  C Education

(1 mark)

QUESTION BANK

SECTION F - RECRUITING AND DEVELOPING EFFECTIVE EMPLOYEES

MIXED QUESTIONS

1   Which two of the following statements about counselling are incorrect?

☐   Counselling helps employees overcome their problems or traumas

☐   Counselling demonstrates to employees that they are valued as individuals

☐   Counselling represents the most common type of "on the job" training

☐   Counselling helps younger, less experienced employees in their career paths

(2 marks)

2   Which of the following is an example of lateral communication?

○   A sales manager assigning individual sales targets to each member of her sales team

○   A production manager sending a report to the purchasing manager outlining all the raw materials he would like to purchase

○   A marketing manager making a presentation to the CEO of his organisation on the features of the company's newest product

○   An employee asking the HR manager of the organisation for a transfer to a different department

(2 marks)

3   Which two of the following are not stages in Kolb's experiential learning cycle?

☐   Applying theory-based principles in real life experiences

☐   Observing others' experiences before starting the activity

☐   Applying conclusions drawn from the experience in new situations

☐   Interpreting and understanding the experience

(2 marks)

4   Which of the following is not one of the purposes of performance appraisal?

○   Identifying areas for improvement

○   Identifying training needs

○   Identifying candidates eligible for promotion

○   Identifying resources to perform tasks

(2 marks)

5   Janima Ltd is recruiting for the post of Accounts Manager. The candidate should be a professionally qualified accountant and a self-motivated individual, having a minimum of five years of relevant experience and a sound practical knowledge of accounting principles. Which of the following includes these details?

○   Job description

○   Person specification

○   Job analysis

(1 mark)

6 Ronald has just gone through a performance appraisal. He has been told that his work has been of an unacceptable quality and if significant improvement is not shown in the next three months he will be dismissed. Which performance appraisal technique has his appraiser used?

○ Tell and sell approach
○ Tell and listen approach
○ Problem solving approach
○ 360 degree approach

(2 marks)

7 Are the following sentences about the patterns of communication true or false?

	True	False
The wheel pattern of communication is the slowest way of communicating	○	○
The chain pattern of communication is the fastest way to send a message	○	○

(2 marks)

8 Effective training and development benefits the organisation by increasing its employee turnover. Is this statement true or false?

○ False
○ True

(1 mark)

9 Which two of the following are causes of ineffective communication?

☐ Unambiguous language
☐ Distorted content
☐ Selective interpretation
☐ Distinct messages

(2 marks)

10 Anna, the production manager, conducted a performance appraisal of Peter, the production worker. Peter was not well during the week before the review, so his work during that week had many errors. As a result, Anna gave him a low rating. What is this type of barrier to effective appraisal known as?

○ The halo effect
○ The recency effect
○ The contrast effect
○ The cluster effect

(2 marks)

11 Which of the following best describes the "pragmatists" learning style as described by Honey and Mumford?

○ Observe first and then choose how to act
○ Enjoy theory or academic based learning
○ Learn through practical experience
○ Learn through practically applying things taught

(2 marks)

12 Which two of the following are not advantages of recruiting from within the organisation?

☐ Provides organisation with a wide source of candidates
☐ Easier to evaluate candidate's suitability for a position
☐ Easier to choose candidates on the basis of their seniority
☐ Candidates are familiar with organisation's culture and processes

(2 marks)

13 The term time management refers to employees strictly adhering to the official work timings of the organisation. Is this statement true or false?

    ○   True

    ○   False

(1 mark)

14 James has learnt how to play a particular song on his piano by watching other piano players on TV. Honey and Mumford would term this style of learning as which of the following?

    ○   Activist

    ○   Pragmatist

    ○   Theorist

    ○   Reflector

(2 marks)

15 John has recently resigned from his position as Assistant Sales Manager of a pharmaceutical company. His organisation has found a replacement and John will spend the next two weeks working with him. This is an example of which of the following?

    ○   Mentoring

    ○   Counselling

    ○   Coaching

    ○   Training

(2 marks)

16 David is currently giving an interview for a position with an organisation. He has the necessary academic qualifications but the organisation wants to determine if he has the appropriate level of knowledge and expertise. Which one of the following testing methods should it use?

    ○   Intelligence test

    ○   Personality test

    ○   Competence test

    ○   Psychometric test

(2 marks)

17 Which of the following is a direct method of recruiting?

    ○   Trade Journals

    ○   Internet

    ○   College campus

    ○   Recruiting agencies

(2 marks)

18 Which of the following is not one of the barriers to effective time management?

    ○   Interruptions

    ○   Frequent meetings

    ○   Procrastinating

    ○   Setting priorities

(2 marks)

19 Which pattern of communication has the disadvantage of offering the sender no feedback?

    ○   The circle

    ○   The chain

    ○   The Y

    ○   The wheel

(2 marks)

20 What do the last two letters in the acronym SMART stand for?

    ☐   Relevant

    ☐   Rational

    ☐   Tactful

    ☐   Timely

(2 marks)

SOLUTION BANK

SECTION A - BUSINESS ORGANISATION STRUCTURE, GOVERNANCE AND MANAGEMENT

SOLUTIONS TO MULTIPLE CHOICE QUESTIONS

1 **B** A customer is an example of a connected stakeholder.

2 **D** Employees often have personal and social relationships with other employees based upon factors other than official reporting lines and duties. So the informal organisation always exists simultaneously with the formal organisation in any organisation.

3 **A** In the context of the Anthony hierarchy, the management level is responsible for setting the initiatives, policies and procedures that will enable the organisation to move in the strategic direction set at the strategic level.

4 **C** Task culture encourages a team approach in the organisation.

5 **C** The matrix organisational structure is suited to very large organisations that operate across multiple countries and/or have multiple product lines.

6 **A** Non executive director serves solely as board member. He does not take an active role in managing the company but is appointed for his or her objectivity in considering the company's affairs and wide experience of business.

7 **D** Good quality information should be relevant i.e. should omit data / details that are not needed, no matter how interesting they are. Good quality information should be economical i.e. the costs of collecting it should always be less than the benefits gained from using it.

8 **A** Decentralisation calls for middle management and operational staff to be granted a limited amount of authority and autonomy so as to encourage them to find solutions to problems as opposed to simply reporting them. Employees can immediately amend an organisation's strategy to changing market conditions instead of having to wait for authorisation to do so.

9 **C** The grapevine represents the way in which information about the company is passed unofficially from employee to employee.

10 **D** The secretary is responsible for communicating the committee decisions to committee members. He does this by minuting the meetings and then circulating these minutes to committee members.

11 **D** Organisations need to establish and maintain corporate governance standards so that the actions and decisions of managers, executives and the board of directors remain ethical, moral and in line with the interests of their shareholders.

12 **D** Centralisation calls for the top management or executives of an organisation to assume all decision making authority. It promotes greater efficiency as it allows an organisation to follow a single focused direction with a high degree of consistency and uniformity. All the other options are advantages of decentralisation.

13 **A** The informal organisation can facilitate team work and cooperation across the organisation. The level of cooperation an employee gets from other employees depends more upon the personal relationship they share than what is officially prescribed.

14 **D** Accountants must at all times remain objective in all their dealings. They must provide truthful and accurate information to give its readers a true and fair picture of the organisation's financial position. Accountants are also expected to follow strictly the code of conduct and ethics laid down by their profession's regulatory body.

15	B	The word "limited" is used for private limited companies because the liability of the owners of the organisation is limited to their investment in the company.
16	B	The time taken for information / suggestions to reach executives from employees is too long resulting in the organisation being slow to respond to environmental changes seen by their front line staff.
17	B	An organisation with a personal culture will be dominated by very strong values and beliefs on the "way things are to be done". Here an organisation structure will exist mainly to support the individual in doing his job.
18	A	The main objective of shareholders is an increase in profitability and thereby an increase in shareholder wealth. So they would like the organisation to charge the highest possible price, as this will mean that they will make more money. However, the organisation's customers would like it to charge the lowest possible price.
19	A	Committees provide a platform for different employees to engage in an open discussion and exchange of ideas to come up with innovative solutions. Committees are time consuming and divided responsibility is one of the disadvantages of committees.
20	A	The IFAC (International Federation of Accountants) through its International Ethics Standards Board for Accountants (IESBA), develops ethical standards and guidance for use by professional accountants and promotes good ethical practices globally. Option B is one of the objectives of the IASB and option C is one of the objectives of the ACCA.
21	D	The marketing mix can be thought of as the mechanics or tactics of marketing. It comprises four components: product, price, place and promotion.
22	B	The interaction between employees will be influenced by the personal relationships they share along with their professional relationships.
23	C	An organisation's marketing function mainly involves determining the needs and demands of customers and delivering products / services to meet those needs and demands.
24	C	The Sarbanes Oxley regulations introduced major changes to the regulation of financial practice and corporate governance. They are intended to increase the reliability of an organisation's financial statements thereby ensuring that they are true and fair.
25	D	Not-for-profit organisations such as universities are started and run for the purpose of providing benefits on an individual level or to society as a whole.
26	C	Business ethics is a branch of ethics that examines rules and principles within a commercial context.
27	B	The audit committee members are typically non-executive directors. The public oversight committee oversees the governance and financial reporting of public organisations. The audit committee reviews internal audit and internal control systems. The remuneration committee determines the remuneration of executive directors.
28	A	Internal stakeholders are closely connected with the organisation and they have a special interest in the organisation's continued existence and growth.
29	D	The main responsibility given to a purchasing department is to procure all the goods or services that the organisation will require in the shortest time and at the lowest price, without compromising on quality.
30	D	Stakeholders with low interest and high power typically are not interested in the organisation's operations but they are capable of influencing the organisation's strategy. Therefore they are kept satisfied by the organisation.
31	B	Experience has shown that being ethical makes good business sense for the organisation in the long run since people are more willing to buy from / work for organisations that have an established reputation for behaving ethically.
32	D	"Nature Care" is Makjem's stakeholder with high interest and low power. It is interested in Makjem's activities but does not have the ability to influence its strategy. Therefore Makjem should keep "Nature Care" informed.

33   **A**   Tall organisations have a much larger number of managerial layers but each manager has a relatively narrow span of control.

34   **D**   The power distance index measures the degree of equality present in a culture. Societies with a low power distance emphasise equality and equal opportunity.

35   **A**   Operational level decisions cover the day-to-day activities of the organisation. Operational information is quantitative, relevant to the short term and obtained from internal sources. Options B and C are characteristics of tactical and strategic information respectively.

36   **A**   Edgar Schein states that the taken-for-granted set of assumptions that are held by the majority of members of an organisation are the principal determinants of its culture. These commonly held assumptions are developed over time and are at the very core of an organisation's culture.

37   **B**   Management information systems typically take raw data from transaction processing systems as input and generate output (reports).

38   **C**   Office automation systems support typical administrative activities and help to increase efficiency and productivity amongst employees when they are processing data and information.

39   **B**   With a divisional structure, an organisation is structured around divisional lines based on the different markets or industries it serves.

40   **A**   Large organisations require a group of employees (their top management) to focus on ensuring that the strategy the organisation is following remains valid. If this group becomes too involved with managerial or operational activities, the strategic direction of the organisation might suffer.

41   **D**   A standing committee is put together to serve a particular function of the organisation on an on-going basis.

42   **B**   These organisations do not have a profit motive but instead aim to provide or deliver a service.

43   **A**   An organisation's culture can be identified as ways behaving and understanding that are shared by employees, referred as "The way we do things around here". Thus it represents and reflects how an organisation operates and functions.

44   **B**   Corporate governance extends to shareholders whereas social responsibility extends to the internal, connected and external stakeholders of the organisation. An organisation needs the support of its stakeholder groups in order to survive and, in turn, it has a social responsibility to help these groups to meet their needs.

45   **B**   The culmination of personal and social relationships that occur when people work in the same environment leads to the creation and existence of the informal organisation.

46   **B**   An auditor's report is not generated by the organisation but by an outside party i.e. auditors.

47   **B**   To ensure good corporate governance, the board of directors needs to meet regularly and be closely involved in the direction and control of the organisation.

48   **A**   Large public limited companies have numerous shareholders who are part owners but are not involved in its operations. Hence to manage the operations of such organisations, there exists a separation between ownership and control.

49   **B**   The function of a direct service provision department is to serve as a single point of contact for an organisation's clients. The administration department serves a purely support function. The finance department is involved in controlling and managing an organisation's money supply.

50   **B**   High uncertainty avoidance indicates a rule-oriented and rigid society. Role culture organisations operate by well-established rules and procedures. This results in a rigid and slow moving organisation.

51   **B**   A committee is formed to deal with a problem or situation that is not the specific responsibility of any one particular person or department.

52   **B**   Professions have a regulatory body that establishes a code of ethics for the profession. This is one of the main conditions that distinguish a profession from an occupation.

SECTION A - BUSINESS ORGANISATION STRUCTURE, GOVERNANCE AND MANAGEMENT

SOLUTIONS TO MIXED QUESTIONS

1 ☑ It results in a rigid organisation
☑ Time taken for suggestions to reach executives is too long

Scalar chain simplifies the roles of all employees as each person has only one boss and there is a clear assignment of duties and responsibilities, and good coordination between the management, supervisors and employees.

2 **A** Apollo organisation [2]

B Dionysus organisation [4]

C Athena organisation [1]

D Zeus organisation [3]

Handy identifies four distinct types of cultural organisations and illustrates their principles through the use of Greek gods.

3 ⦿ A manual system is cheaper and faster to implement

Manual systems are easier, faster and cheaper for an organisation to implement.

4 ⦿ Can be viewed as investment

CSR not only involves compliance with legislation but also acting in a socially responsible manner and serving society by giving "something back". CSR can be viewed as investment and is in the long-term interests of shareholders because it helps to secure stakeholder support and sustainable business relationships.

5 **A** Decision support system [3]

B Office automation system [4]

C Management information system [1]

D Transaction processing system [2]

6 ⦿ All are false

Stakeholders with a high level of power but low interest are of medium importance to an organisation. Stakeholders with low interest and power are of low importance to the organisation. Stakeholders with high interest and a high level of power are most important to an organisation.

7 ⊙ (i) Legality (ii) Morality

Legality because ethics involves obeying the laws of a country. Morality because ethics involves doing what a society believes is just and correct.

8 ⊙ False

The culture of the organisation is likely to be more diverse when more minorities, ethnic groups and nationalities are present in its workforce.

9 ⊙ Ad-hoc committee

Ad-hoc committees are put together to respond to particular situation or to address a particular need in the organisation. They are typically dissolved once their purpose has been served.

10 ⊙ Office automation system

Office automation systems represent a combination of hardware, software and networks to enable employees to perform traditional paper-based tasks electronically.

11 ⊙ Informal communication

The flow of information is informal. If the manager directly passes on information to the employees then it is considered formal communication.

12 ☑ The external environment
   ☑ Macroeconomic factors and demographic patterns

Information on the performance of an organisation's workforce and past sales data is required to make tactical decisions.

13

	Flat organisation	Tall organisation
Tom	○	⊙
Dick	⊙	○

Tall organisations have much larger numbers of managerial layers, which implies a narrow span of control. The roles and responsibilities of all the employees are typically well defined. Flat organisations have fewer managerial layers, which implies a wide span of control. A much greater level of independence is given to each employee.

14 ⊙ Low uncertainty avoidance

Low uncertainty avoidance indicates a society that is not rule-oriented and has greater tolerance for a variety of ideas, thoughts and beliefs.

15 ⊙ True

This helps ensure that non-executive directors hold the management accountable for their actions, remain objective when setting organisational strategy, and make independent judgments about management performance.

16 ⊙ A

Stakeholders with a high interest but low power such as community representatives are of medium importance to an organisation. They should be kept informed by the organisation even though they cannot influence its strategy.

17 ⊙ None of them

Tactical decisions are taken at the management level. Executives decide where the organisation should strive to be in the future. Operational staff is involved in the day-to-day aspects of running the business.

18 ☑ Managers
☑ Employees

Shareholders are the owners of a limited company and are connected stakeholders. Partners are the internal stakeholders of a partnership firm. Executive and non-executive directors are not involved in company's day to day operations. Their main role instead is to set the long term objectives and strategy and oversee the functioning of the company. So, they are connected stakeholders. Customers are also connected stakeholders.

19 ⦿ Departmental

Structuring the organisation in line with customer needs creates a departmental structure. Billing & enquiry, marketing, after sales service, etc. are all departments based on customer needs.

20 ☑ Reviewing organisation's financial statements and internal control
☑ Appointing the external auditors and determining their remuneration

An audit committee oversees the work of the organisation's internal auditors to ensure the overall integrity of the organisation's financial statements. It is also involved in managing relationships with an organisation's external auditors and reviewing an organisation's internal control.

21 ⦿ (i) only

An informal organisation is not always destructive and unreliable. It can build a sense of motivation and co-operation amongst employees. An informal organisation arises out of the personal relationships and communication links that naturally occur amongst employees, but its purpose is not to help the organisation achieve its objectives. It can either help or hinder the management in implementing policies and procedures.

22 ☑ Creating value to customers
☑ Delivering value to customers
☑ Communicating value to customers
☑ Managing customer relationships
☑ Market segmentation
☑ Market research

Controlling money supply is a finance function and ensuring overall day-to-day functioning of the organisation is an administrative function.

23 ☑ Transparency
☑ Reliability

Transparency and reliability are the personal qualities expected in an accountant.

24

	Yes	No
Entrepreneurial	⦿	○
Product	⦿	○

Entrepreneurial structure is found in small owner / operated firms. The roles and tasks of the employees are decided by the owner on an ad-hoc basis in this type of structure. In a product structure, an organisation divides itself along its product lines. This type of structure is often followed by organisations that make multiple products.

25 ⦿ False

An informal organisation always exists simultaneously along with a formal one. Informal groups occur in an organisation because of the personal relationships that develop between employees.

26 ⦿ A large traditional corporate

A role culture is one where the organisation works in accordance with well detailed procedures, role descriptions and authority definitions. Large traditional corporates typically have this kind of culture.

27 ⦿ Standing committee

A standing committee operates on an on-going basis, almost like a department in an organisation. Given that auditing is an on-going function in an organisation, an audit committee will be a standing committee.

28 ⊙ Unethical

Though employing child labour is legal in the country where Loweita has a factory, use of child labour is morally wrong. Ethics involves doing what is right and what will not harm the interest of others. It refers to abiding by a set of written and unwritten rules based not only on legality but on morality as well.

29 ⊙ False

Ethics does not provide a single clear cut direction for people to follow. It only provides a way through which people can evaluate their decisions and / or behaviour.

30 ⊙ Non executive directors

Many new regulations such as the Sarbanes Oxley Act have increased the accountability of non-executive directors of an organisation.

SOLUTION BANK

SECTION B – KEY ENVIRONMENTAL INFLUENCES AND CONSTRAINTS ON BUSINESS AND ACCOUNTING

SOLUTIONS TO MULTIPLE CHOICE QUESTIONS

1 A Political, economic, social and technological factors are the environmental forces that shape and influence the external environment an organisation operates in.

2 C 'Technological advances' is not one of the five forces identified by Porter that influence how competitive an industry is.

3 C Fiscal policy focuses on setting the level of public expenditure, public borrowing and taxation to manage the total demand for goods and services in an economy.

4 B A country's political system and government policy set the rules and regulations of the external environment that all organisations must operate in. This affects the choices that an organisation can and does make.

5 B A sunrise industry is an industry which is in the growth stage. Therefore, typically, competition is not intense between firms as the market is sufficiently large and growing.

6 C A decreasing birth rate and a decreasing death rate have resulted in many societies in which the elderly form the most populous age group.

7 C The Data Protection Act is formulated to protect the individual. The terms of the Act do not cover data about corporate entities.

8 B For businesses, demand for the goods and services they produce will decline. This translates into either lower wages or fewer work opportunities for individuals which in turn translate into lower incomes for households.

9 A When a country imports more than its exports, it creates a balance of payments deficit. This is because the flow of money out of the country is higher than the flow of money into the country.

10 D In the case of high price inflation, the value of money reduces consistently over time. The debts lose 'real value' with inflation. A country's exports become relatively expensive and imports relatively cheap compared to other countries. For individuals with fixed income, their incomes will buy lower amounts of goods and services than before.

11 B The profits will be lower as firms will attempt to outdo others by offering lower prices and/or higher quality.

12 C The "stag" part of the term relates to stagnant or declining GDP whilst the "flation" segment refers to the rising prices of goods and services.

13 B Full employment, price stability, economic growth and balance of payments equilibrium are the four main macro-economic policy objectives.

14 B There is an onus on both the individual and the organisation to maintain the security of data. The law requires that individuals and employees who are not authorised to access any information should recognise and comply with this fact.

15 C A country experiences economic growth when its Gross Domestic Product (GDP) rises. GDP measures the annual output of a country.

16 B Outsourcing can bring the benefits of economies of scale. Organisations often outsource non-core business activities to third party (such as payroll, accounting and customer service) so that they can focus on their core business.

17   **A**   An increase in the money supply results in increased demand for goods and services, which ultimately is reflected in higher prices for these goods and services.

18   **B**   During a deflationary period, the prices of goods and services decrease over time. Therefore consumers are typically better off delaying their purchases.

19   **B**   Direct discrimination is said to occur when a person is treated less favourably than others because of factors such as his gender, race or marital status.

20   **A**   Social factors represent changing consumer tastes and preferences and overall societal trends. In recent times, society in general has become more environmentally conscious.

21   **A**   Governments often raise interest rates to combat inflation because the increased rate acts as an incentive for people to save their money rather than spend it on goods and services. This has the effect of driving down demand and consequently the price of goods and services.

22   **C**   Downsizing is said to occur when a large number of employees are no longer required by the organisation.

23   **D**   GDP (Gross Domestic Product) measures the total value of all the goods and services that a country produces.

24   **D**   Social structure divides society into three main classes: upper class, middle class and working class. People from each class typically have similar tastes and buying patterns. Therefore changes in a country's social structure will also result in changes in the level of demand they have for an organisation's goods or services.

25   **B**   Delayering refers to reducing the number of managerial layers in an organisation. The underlying belief is that a flatter structure will result in a less bureaucratic and faster moving organisation.

26   **D**   All the three options are the reasons why organisations need to maintain health and safety in the workplace

27   **D**   Trade unions often lobby political parties to introduce legislation that favours employees.

28   **B**   Import duties or quotas on foreign goods make foreign goods more expensive for consumers and reduce the demand for them. This helps in reducing a balance of payments deficit.

29   **B**   Most countries are divided into separate regions. Each region has its own regional legal authority or government and a national legal authority or government exists for the nation as a whole.

30   **A**   A supra-national body comprises a number of member nations. Its main aim is to govern the relationship that exists between these nations and settle any dispute that may arise between two or more member nations. The United Nations is an example of a supra-national body that settles political disputes that occur between countries.

31   **D**   The recent trend of western companies giving business to Indian IT companies has arisen because the services provided by Indian IT companies are more competitively priced. Therefore, the loss of business for the UK consultancy firm is due to an economic factor.

32   **A**   A decrease in the rate of unemployment will result in an increase in the rate of inflation and an increase in the rate of unemployment will result in a decrease in the rate of inflation. An increase in the unemployment rate results in consumers having less money to buy the same set of goods and services thereby causing their prices to fall and vice-versa.

33   **C**   The average income rate is an economic factor.

34   **C**   Delayering reduces the number of managerial layers in an organisation thereby allowing it to have a flatter structure.

35   **A**   A consultancy business has very low capital cost requirements which in turn means that there are very few barriers to entry. If there are few barriers to entry, the potential threat of new entrants is high.

SOLUTION BANK

SOLUTIONS TO MIXED QUESTIONS

1 ☑ Treating all employees equally
☑ Protecting employees from unfair termination
☑ Protecting employees from discrimination

One of the main purposes of the law, with regard to the individual and employment, is to ensure that organisations treat all employees equally. The law attempts to protect individuals from discrimination and unfair termination.

2 ☑ To achieve a balance between a country's imports and exports
☑ To achieve stable prices

To achieve full employment is one of the four macro-economic policy objectives of a government. Full employment doesn't mean all people are employed, but it means that unemployment levels are low. To achieve economic growth is one of the four macro-economic policy objectives,; maximising economic growth is not one of these objectives..

3 ⦿ Downgrading

Delayering refers to reducing the number of managerial layers in an organisation. Outsourcing refers to contracting certain activities to third party. Downsizing refers to reducing the number of employees in an organisation. All these are effects of technological changes in organisational structure and strategy.

4 ⦿ Increase public expenditure

Governments very often increase public expenditure in times of high unemployment. This increased expenditure results in increased income for many organisations which in turn leads to their expanding and recruiting more labour.

5

	True	False
It is high when the cost of switching to an alternative supplier is high	○	⦿
It is low when there is a concentration of buyers	○	⦿

The bargaining power of buyers is low when the cost of switching for the customer is high, and it is high when there is a concentration of buyers.

6 ⦿ True

Social trends influence the purchase decisions that an individual makes. A business's outcome depends on the level of goods and services it sells, and the condition of the economy depends on the total level of demand that exists for its goods and services.

7 ⦿ Information should be maintained for at least ten years

The law with regard to data security states that confidential information on employees should be held for no longer than necessary.

8 ☑ Legal
☑ Political

"Introduction of new taxes" represents a political factor and "changes in employment laws" represents a legal factor. Political factors are caused by the role that the government plays in shaping the environment the organisation operates in. Legal factors represent the legislative framework within which the organisation must operate.

9 ◉ Structural unemployment

If the skill set of individuals working in an industry does not change in accordance with the changes in the structure of that industry, then they will no longer be able to work in that industry.

10 ◉ Direct discrimination

Gender restriction is a form of direct discrimination. Direct discrimination occurs when a person is treated less favourably than others in situations such as recruitment, selection or employment, because of factors such as gender, race or marital status.

11 ☑ There is an inverse relationship between interest rate and the level of public expenditure
   ☑ The key objective of monetary policy is achieving price stability

Monetary policy involves controlling the supply or level of money in an economy. Fiscal policy involves managing aggregate demand in the economy.

12 ◉ Taxation rates

Governments use taxes to achieve their social objective of reducing the income and wealth gap between different classes within a society. Typically, the upper-class sections of society are taxed at higher rates than the middle or lower classes. Much of this tax is then spent on providing subsidised goods and services to the less privileged.

13 ◉ Delayering

Delayering refers to reducing the number of managerial layers in an organisation. This causes the organisation to assume a "flatter" structure.

14 ◉ Competitive rivalry

Competitive rivalry is intense in the airline industry. Fixed costs are so high that airlines need to fill as many seats as possible for a scheduled flight even if some of the seats are sold at discounted prices.

SOLUTION BANK

SOLUTIONS TO MULTIPLE CHOICE QUESTIONS

1 A Investors use financial information to assess the economic performance and financial condition of the company. Therefore, the accounting policies and financial statements of companies are expected to be relevant to investment and financing decisions, and reliable and comparable with other companies.

2 B Despite the benefits of automation in business and financial systems, organisations still need to ensure that a system of checks and controls is implemented and maintained to ensure the organisation continues to operate effectively and efficiently.

3 D The main role of the accounting department is providing reliable, relevant, complete and accurate financial information to the users.

4 A Determining the product price is the financial issue associated with marketing. Accounting for all the goods returned to a supplier is the financial issue associated with purchasing.

5 A The organisation takes into account the size, reputation and financial stability of its customers but not of the other companies customers deal with when deciding the credit level to be granted to them.

6 A The law requires organisations to maintain proper records and financial accounts, as they have to pay taxes on any profits they make.

7 A In 1494 an Italian mathematician, Luca Pacioli, in his book 'Suma', introduced the 'double entry' book-keeping system (the foundation or cornerstone of accounting).

8 D A working capital management system should ensure that there is always a sufficient level of working capital to meet the cost of its operating requirements until the time it receives payments from its customers.

9 D The IASB aims to promote consistency in corporate reporting by developing a single set of high quality, enforceable and global accounting standards.

10 B Accounting information provides information about past events. For the purpose of decision making, the past is used as a guide for future estimates of the consequences of different alternatives.

11 C Microsoft Excel is a proprietary spreadsheet application written and distributed by Microsoft. All the other options are examples of database systems.

12 C The treasury represents the function of managing an organisation's money supply. This function is either performed by a dedicated department or becomes the responsibility of the finance department.

13 C In order for an organisation to become listed on a stock exchange, it must maintain and report a high level a detail of financial information on itself. This allows investors to make informed investment decisions.

14 C One aim of a purchasing control system is to ensure that all credits are duly paid. Meeting the monthly sales targets set by the top management is not an aim of the financial control system which relates to sales.

15 C A computerised system is more accurate and reliable than a manual system. One disadvantage of using a manual system is the increased effort that it requires from accountants. The advantages of using a computerised system include easy back-up and restoration of records.

SOLUTION BANK

SOLUTIONS TO MIXED QUESTIONS

1 ☑ Allows users to run various "what if" scenarios
     ☑ Allows users to use shortcuts when performing mathematical calculations

These two are the features of a spreadsheet application.

2 ☑ Tax liability
     ☑ Level of profits

An annual return is a statement submitted by the organisation to the government that denotes the financial condition of the organisation, the level of profits earned by the business and the corresponding tax liability.

3 ⦿ (ii) and (iii)

Preparing a marketing strategy and deciding payment terms with outside vendors are not financial issues concerned with accounting.

4 ☑ All the orders for purchases are properly authorised
     ☑ All the purchases are recorded accurately

Orders are placed only with the authorised suppliers who supply goods of the required quality at competitive prices. Only the purchases that have been ordered and properly authorised are accepted and paid for.

5 ⦿ Payslip

A payslip is an output of a payroll system.

6

	True	False
It is faster to develop than the manual financial system.	○	⦿
It secures data better than the manual financial system.	○	⦿

Computerised systems are more time-consuming to develop and implement than the manual systems. Like manual systems, computerised systems are also subject to the loss of data, damage and unauthorised access. Appropriate data security measures need to be provided for computerised systems.

SOLUTION BANK

SECTION D - SPECIFIC FUNCTIONS OF ACCOUNTING AND INTERNAL FINANCIAL CONTROL

SOLUTIONS TO MULTIPLE CHOICE QUESTIONS

1	A	One of the main responsibilities of the treasury function is risk management. Risk management refers to mitigating or minimising an organisation's interest rate risk and foreign exchange risk.
2	B	The internal auditor would only be responsible for evaluating the effectiveness and efficiency of an organisation's internal control system.
3	B	Adding value and improving the client's operations is the internal auditor's objective. The external auditor is responsible for reporting on the accuracy and fairness of the organisation's financial statements to its shareholders and not on its financial performance.
4	C	It is the duty of an external auditor to submit a report on the truth and fairness of an organisation's financial statements and express an opinion on whether they are free of material misstatements.
5	B	Working capital is calculated as current assets minus current liabilities. Working capital management refers to maintaining a level of capital which is sufficient to meet the cost of the organisation's operating requirements. It involves managing the organisation's short-term assets and short-term liabilities such as inventory, accounts receivable and accounts payable.
6	B	The implementation of a system of checks and balances is the responsibility of the accounting department of an organisation.
7	C	The treasury department is responsible for managing an organisation's money supply. It has to ensure that the organisation has sufficient capital to fund its operations and place any excess money into viable investment options.
8	B	The controls associated with an internal control system can be classified as accounting controls and administrative controls.
9	C	These situations involve misappropriation of cash. In situation (iii) an employee deliberately overstates a payment that is to be made to a supplier and in situation (iv) an employee deliberately understates a payment received from a supplier. In both cases the employees take home the excess amounts.
10	A	Product mix decisions involve deciding which products are profitable and should continue to be offered and deciding the combination of products to be offered by the organisation. Management accounting provides information for making product mix decisions.
11	D	Fraud in accounting and business is said to occur when an organisation intentionally misstates its financial performance and position. This may occur either because of fraudulent financial records and reporting or because the assets of an organisation have been misappropriated (misused or stolen).
12	C	An external auditor will be mainly concerned about whether the internal control system prevents and/or detects errors in recording financial information. External auditors can rely on an organisation's internal controls to determine how much substantive audit work must be done. Strong internal controls will require less audit work and weak internal controls will require more audit work.

13 **A** In a case of teeming and lading, the receipt from one customer is misappropriated. In order to keep the account 'moving', the receipt from the second customer is posted to the account of the first customer; the receipt from the third customer is posted to the account of the second customer and so forth.

14 **B** The main aim of internal checks is to prevent fraud and errors rather than to detect them. They are designed to ensure that malpractices such as fraud or theft do not occur.

15 **B** A systems audit is concerned with ensuring the efficiency and effectiveness of internal controls within an organisation.

16 **B** Management accounting provides the executives and managers of an organisation with a variety of information they can use when making operational and/or investment decisions.

17 **D** An external auditor is appointed by the shareholders of an organisation. He is accountable to the shareholders and his reports are submitted to them.

18 **B** Encryption involves transforming stored data into a coded or encrypted format each time it is sent from one computer to another. The encrypted data is meaningless to any reader until it is decoded by the receiving computer.

19 **D** Whistle-blowing is not a consequence of fraud but one of the measures to detect fraud. A number of countries provide a framework of legal protection for 'whistleblowers" i.e. employees who expose malpractice or fraud in an organisation.

20 **D** Physical access to an organisation's systems / software can be controlled by measures such as keeping all IT equipment in a secure area e.g. a room that has door lock or a card locking system.

21 **B** Merely designing an effective internal control system will not reduce the possibility of fraud in an organisation. It needs to be implemented efficiently throughout the organisation. The system should also be regularly reviewed in the light of changing circumstances; otherwise it may lose its significance and effectiveness.

22 **A** The finance function is mainly responsible for evaluating and obtaining finance and managing the working capital of an organisation. Budgeting and budgetary control is the role of management accounting. Reporting on an organisation's state of affairs is the role of financial accounting.

23 **B** A statement of comprehensive income has two components: revenues and expenses. Revenues represent the assets generated (such as cash) from the sale of goods or services over a particular period. Expenses represent the costs the organisation has incurred in the same period.

24 **A** Application controls are controls that prevent, detect, and correct errors in transactions as they flow through the various stages of a specific business or data processing system.

25 **A** The management should always closely monitor the business environment in which the organisation operates. Such monitoring will alert the management to unusual events or indicators of potential fraud that occur in the business environment.

26 **C** Fraud involves the misappropriation of assets. The most commonly misappropriated asset is cash and therefore fraud is most likely to occur in the sales department which receives and remits cash frequently.

27 **C** Timely, reliable and accurate financial reporting, effective and efficient conducting of operations and compliance with all applicable laws and regulations are the three main objectives of internal control.

28 **C** The management accountant provides information for making operational and/or investment decisions including rent or buy decisions.

29 **A** The three main accounting functions are recording financial information (recognition), codifying and processing financial information (measurement) and preparing financial statements (presentation).

30 **B** Mitigating business tax liabilities is a legal activity as it involves reducing the tax liability by applying legitimate rules. This is one of the main finance functions within the organisation.

31 **A** Substantive tests are used to verify the accounting figures and the accuracy of the financial information. Compliance tests are used to obtain audit evidence about the operating effectiveness of internal controls.

32 **D** Some of the procedures used by internal and external auditors are very similar.

33 **A** Safeguarding of assets is an example of an accounting control which in turn is a part of an organisation's internal control system.

34 **A** System recovery procedures recover / restore the system in the event of system failure / breakdown.

35 **B** The investors making investment decisions based on the misleading financial statements of the company will eventually find that the actual returns are less than the expected returns since the company's financial performance is overstated.

36 **D** Accounting controls call for the implementation of a control system where inventory is regularly physically verified and compared with the book balance to ensure that no inventory is stolen or becomes obsolete.

SOLUTION BANK

SECTION D - SPECIFIC FUNCTIONS OF ACCOUNTING AND INTERNAL FINANCIAL CONTROL

SOLUTIONS TO MIXED QUESTIONS

1

A	Cash fraud	3	(Overstating a payment that has to be made)
B	Asset fraud	2	(Using organisation's asset for personal purposes)
C	Manipulation of financial statements	1	(Manipulation of stock valuation)

2   ☑ Password
　　 ☑ Firewall
　　 ☑ Network access control

A password is a string of characters which helps to prevent unauthorised users from accessing a system or data resource. A firewall prevents outsiders from accessing an organisation's private networks and private data resources connected to the Internet, especially intranets. Network access control restricts unauthorised access to an organisation's computer network by restricting the availability of network resources. An audit trail keeps an exact record of when each computer was used, which employee it was used by and which operations they performed.

3   ☑ External auditors are required by law to be professionally qualified accountants
　　 ☑ External auditors report to the shareholders of a company

External auditors are appointed by the shareholders. They are mainly concerned with submitting a report on the truth and fairness of an organisation's financial statements.

4   ⦿ Compliance test

Compliance tests are used to obtain audit evidence about the operating effectiveness of internal controls.

5   **A**   4

　　 B   3

　　 C   1

　　 D   2

6   ☑   Accountants
     ☑   Managers
     ☑   Internal auditor
     ☑   Board of directors

The ultimate responsibility for preventing and detecting fraudulent practices and malpractices in an organisation is that of its board of directors. All individual managers are expected to be involved in the fraud detection and removal process along with accountants and internal auditors. They should be alert to the possibility that unusual events or transactions could be indicators of fraud or attempted fraud.

7   **Yes**   **No**

An organisation's inventory is damaged as a result of flooding   ⦿   ○
An organisation purchases a fleet of new vehicles   ○   ⦿

An event in accounting terminology is an incident that monetarily affects the organisation. The purchase of a fleet of vehicles can be classified as a "transaction".

8   ☑   Inventory valuation and reporting
     ☑   Budgeting, budgetary control and variance analysis

Working capital management and risk assessment are finance and treasury functions. Purchase ledger, sales invoicing and payroll are financial accounting functions.

9   **True**   **False**

Internal auditors are always employees of an organisation.   ○   ⦿
Internal auditors report to the shareholders.   ○   ⦿

Internal auditors are usually employees of an organisation but sometimes the management may outsource the internal audit function. Internal auditors report to the board of directors or audit committee.

10   ⦿   Authorising, recording and custody

The internal check of "segregation of duties" calls for the tasks of authorising a transaction, recording the transaction and taking physical custody of the asset obtained through the transaction to be performed by different people. This reduces the possibilities of errors or malpractices such as fraud, misappropriation and thefts.

11   ☑   A system of adequate internal checks
     ☑   Explicit directives on the roles and responsibility of employees

Management override and collusion among employees are limitations on the effectiveness of an internal financial control procedure. Internal control proves to be ineffective when management decides to circumvent it. There is a possibility of escaping from controls through employees colluding among themselves or with outside parties.

12   ⦿   Performance-based reward system for managers

The existence of a reward system for managers that is based on their performance increases the pressure on the managers and acts as an incentive for them to manipulate performance / results. All the other options reduce the possibility of fraud in an organisation.

SOLUTION BANK

SECTION E - LEADING AND MANAGING INDIVIDUALS AND TEAMS

SOLUTIONS TO MULTIPLE CHOICE QUESTIONS

1   **C**   Leaders with a task motivation personality will be more effective in an organisation with a formalised hierarchical structure.

2   **D**   According to Belbin's team roles theory, a shaper is a very task-focused individual who is committed to the team achieving its objectives. He usually "shapes" the behaviour of others to work towards achieving the team objectives.

3   **C**   SMART objectives stand for objectives which are Specific, Measurable, Achievable, Realistic and Time-related.

4   **A**   In Maslow's hierarchy of needs, self-actualisation needs represent the top level of needs, which are also termed growth needs. Morality, spirituality and acceptance are examples of such needs.

5   **C**   Tuckman's team development theory describes and explains how a team develops over the time. Tuckman identified five stages of development that teams go through over the course of their lives, which are forming, storming, norming, performing and adjourning.

6   **B**   According to the Ashridge model, the autocratic style of leader makes all the decisions and issues the instructions that must be followed by subordinates. The democratic leader gives the most decision making powers to subordinates.

7   **C**   The more agreeable the individual is, the more likely he is to get along with others and fit into the culture of the organisation.

8   **B**   The scientific theory of management states that most workers work at a productivity rate that is well below their potential. Hence a manager has to be responsible for every aspect of his subordinate's job right from the design of the job up to how it is performed.

9   **B**   Statement A was made by Fayol in his classical theory of management. Statement B was made by Taylor in his scientific theory of management. The statement C was made by Mayo. Statement D was made by Drucker in his "management by objectives" theory.

10   **B**   Project teams are put together for the sole purpose of working on one specific project. Typically members come from a range of backgrounds and have a variety of expertise.

11   **C**   According to Herzberg, people's satisfaction and dissatisfaction levels in regards to their work are caused by different sets of factors. He classified these factors into two categories: motivators and hygiene factors.

12   **A**   Leader position power refers to the power the leader automatically has because of his position. Task structure refers to how routine, standardised and easy to monitor the tasks of a leader's subordinates are. Leader-member relation represents the personal relationships that a leader has with the members of his group.

13   **A**   The main purposes of a team are to provide the structure or the framework necessary to coordinate the efforts of several individuals and the team also helps to meet the psychological needs of the team members through social interaction.

14   **A**   According to Maslow, the first and most important set of needs that people want to satisfy is their "physiological" or base needs. These include needs such as breathing, food and water.

15   **C**   The main difference between a group and a team is that groups only share a common purpose whereas teams have a specific goal to achieve.

16   **B**   According to Drucker, the activity trap occurs when managers get too involved or "hands-on" with the day-to-day activities of their function or department and end up becoming more like employees.

17   C   The three main factors that influence group behaviour are the composition of the group, the size of the group and the group's norms. Group location is not very likely to influence group behaviour.

18   A   According to Belbin's team roles theory, a team worker is a very diplomatic individual. He focuses on ensuring the team functions effectively as a whole and personal conflicts between individual members are minimised.

19   A   A group functions efficiently if it is cohesive. Members are likely to be more focused on the task at hand.

20   B   A 9.9 leadership style on Blake and Mounton's managerial grid represents high concern for people and high concern for production. This type of leader gets work accomplished from committed people and develops a relationship of trust and respect with them.

21   C   At the norming stage, the roles and responsibilities of individual members are clarified. In addition, rules, values, acceptable behaviours and work styles start to get established for the team.

22   B   According to D. McGregor's X-Y theory of management, theory Y is a participative style of management. It assumes that the average person doesn't dislike work inherently. He / she can be made to learn to not only accept but seek responsibility.

23   D   According to Belbin's team roles theory, a plant represents a very creative and imaginative individual who focuses on problem solving and addressing the major issues facing the team.

24   D   Management of meaning refers to the ability of leaders to transform their vision into reality. Leaders should be effective communicators and get others to follow their vision.

25   D   According to Belbin, three people-oriented roles team members adopt are: coordinator (a very people-oriented individual), team worker (a very diplomatic individual) and resource investigator (a very enthusiastic and extrovert individual).

26   A   The main characteristic of team is that its members share a specific performance goal for which they are all accountable.

27   A   Leadership involves setting a clear direction for people to follow. Supervision involves directly overseeing and assisting people when they are performing their assigned tasks. Leadership requires the lowest level of involvement and interaction with people. Supervision requires the highest level of involvement and interaction with people.

28   C   Individuals with achievement motivation are motivated to achieve for the sake of the feeling of accomplishment they get when they achieve their goals.

29   B   Interpersonal roles involve the social or personal aspects of a manager's job. Informational roles involve the receiving, handling, processing and reporting of data that flows in and out of a manager's department. Decisional roles involve managers taking decisions on behalf of their department or function.

30   B   To be effective, teams must have an attachment to a "superordinate" or higher goal. Teams tend to function and perform better when have been given challenging goals.

31   C   Planning refers to deciding what objectives are going to be met as well as what activities must be carried out to meet these objectives. Any action that has to be taken has to be pre-planned.

32   C   One of the three main principles of the human relations school theory is that individuals perform better when empowered.

33   B   A group can be defined as "two or more persons who interact with one another such that each person influences and is influenced by each other person". This condition is satisfied only in the case of the eight employees who work for the same department.

34   B   A salary is one of the top six hygiene factors identified by Herzberg. According to his motivation-hygiene theory, hygiene factors are the factors that have the potential to cause employee dissatisfaction.

SOLUTION BANK

SOLUTIONS TO MIXED QUESTIONS

1 ☑ Work conditions
☑ Salary
☑ Relationship with boss
☑ Company policy

Hygiene factors represent the bare minimum set of conditions that an organisation needs to ensure are in place for its employees. Motivators, in contrast, represent factors that enrich an employee's job and therefore cause his motivation levels to increase. Thus responsibilities, career progression, growth and recognition are motivators and not hygiene factors.

2 ⊙ Implementer

According to Belbin's team roles theory, implementers are efficient and practical individuals who focus on turning ideas into practical actions.

3 **A** Decisional ☐ 3

B Informational ☐ 1

C Interpersonal ☐ 2

The disseminator represents the role of disseminating relevant information to subordinates. He falls under the informational roles category. The figurehead represents the role of performing ceremonial duties. He falls under the interpersonal roles category. The negotiator represents the role of negotiating with both inside and outside parties. He falls under the decisional roles category.

4 ☑ Interact with each other
☑ Influence each other

A group is defined as "two or more persons who interact with one another such that each person influences and is influenced by each other person". However, to be defined as a group, a collection of people need not necessarily share similar characteristics or work styles.

5 ⊙ Performing

At the performing stage, the team is functioning as a cohesive whole with no interference or participation from the leader. The team is focused on and works towards achieving its goals and objectives.

6 ☑ Group needs
☑ Individual needs
☑ Task needs

The "contingency approach" developed by Adair states that the effectiveness of a leader is contingent upon his ability to meet task needs (the need to achieve the common task), group needs (the need to be held together as a group) and the individual needs of various individuals group members.

7 ◉ (i) and (iv)

Working in teams helps individuals to avoid wasted efforts and reduces errors thereby leading to greater productivity and better performance. The use of teams also develops a sense of coordination and cooperation across the organisation. The development of social relationships is not an advantage of the use of teams by an organisation. Reaching a consensus on decisions can be slow in teams because of differences of opinion between members.

8 ☑ A high concern for people
☑ A low concern for production

Managers with a high concern for people but a low concern for production are labelled "country club" managers by Blake and Mouton as their main concern is for the well-being of their staff even if it is at the expense of productivity and results.

9 ◉ Informal group

The reason for forming an informal group is usually non-work-related such as friendship or a common interest.

10 ◉ Scientific theory of management

The scientific theory of management states that most workers work at a productivity rate that is well below their potential. Managers must therefore scientifically study all jobs and processes and develop a standardised method for performing each one.

11 ◉ Division of authority

Fayol's 14 principles of management include the principle of "division of work" which states that division increases output by making employees more efficient. The principle of "unity of command" states that each employee should have only one boss. The principle of "Esprit de corps" states the need for promoting team spirit, unity and harmony among employees. The principle of "discipline" states that all employees should strictly obey organisation's rules.

12 ☑ Action
☑ People
☑ Cerebral

Belbin identified nine clusters of behaviours or "team roles" that individuals play. These nine roles are categorised as action-oriented roles, people-oriented roles and cerebral-oriented roles.

13 ☑ Monitor Evaluator
☑ Plant
☑ Specialist

Monitor evaluator, plant and specialist are all cerebral-oriented roles whereas implementer, completer, resource investigator and shaper are all action-oriented roles.

14 **A** Belonging needs   `2`

    B Self-actualisation needs   `3`

    C Physiological needs   `4`

    D Esteem needs   `1`

15 ◉ Materiality

Vroom's theory states that Motivation = Expectancy x (Valence x Instrumentality).

16 ☑ High interpersonal conflicts

☑ Reactive problem solving approach

Interpersonal conflicts between team members are low in effective teams. The approach to problem solving is proactive.

17 ⊙ X

According to D. McGregor's X-Y theory of management, theory X is an authoritarian style of management and suggests that most people dislike work and responsibility and will avoid doing any if they can.

18 ☑ High morale
☑ Job satisfaction

Intrinsic rewards arise from carrying out the particular activity rather than any results that may arise out of completion of the activity. The other two options are extrinsic rewards.

SOLUTION BANK

SOLUTIONS TO MULTIPLE CHOICE QUESTIONS

1   **D**   A mentor is a role model who guides another employee. Mentors are usually older and more experienced members of an organisation. Their responsibility is to help younger, less experienced members of the organisation on their career paths.

2   **B**   Noise can be defined as any factor that interferes with the communication of the message and/or its corresponding feedback.

3   **B**   Theorists represent people who enjoy theory or academic based learning. They prefer to understand principles.

4   **C**   Counselling refers to the discussions an employee has with another individual (typically a professional counsellor) in relation to a personal problem he or she is facing. These problems are normally emotional rather than work-related.

5   **B**   Personality tests attempt to measure the basic aspects of a person's personality.

6   **D**   The wheel pattern of communication is the most effective communication method, mainly because a sender can communicate directly with each group member.

7   **B**   Interviews are very subjective in nature. Factors such as personal affinity with the candidate may affect the interviewer's judgment about the candidate.

8   **D**   Selective interpretation occurs when the receiver purposely interprets a message to suit his purpose.

9   **B**   The halo effect represents the tendency of a reviewer to rate the overall performance of an employee on just one factor or aspect.

10   **B**   Informal channels represent the way employees like to communicate with each other. They occur spontaneously and are used by employees to exchange ideas, information and views.

11   **A**   The position of mail-delivery person does not require a high qualification and requires someone from the same locality. It is very unlikely that prospective candidates for this type of vacancy would search for an opening in a professional magazine or register with a recruitment agency.

12   **A**   The "buddy" system involves employees from different departments teaming up to help each other meet their respective objectives.

13   **A**   Development is the term used to describe the activities an individual will undertake to help him not only improve his current job performance but also to gain broader knowledge and skills.

14   **C**   In the problem solving approach, the employee is encouraged to come up with ways and solutions that will improve his job performance or any problems he is encountering. The reviewer also provides his inputs so that a set of mutually acceptable improvement goals can be decided upon.

15   **C**   The second step in the training and development process is to set out specific and measurable knowledge and performance objectives based on the gaps or deficiencies identified for potential learners.

16   B   The equal opportunities policy states that an organisation should ensure that all employees are treated equally. Employees should only be judged and evaluated on their work and integrity and not on other factors such as race, religion or gender.

17   A   Performance appraisals measure whether an employee did or did not do what was expected of him. Therefore by seeing if the people who are hired by the organisation are performing in their jobs, the effectiveness of the organisation's recruitment and selection process can be evaluated.

18   B   In a chain pattern of communication, each group member communicates only with the person adjoining him. This type of communication pattern is quite common in a highly hierarchical and formal organisation.

19   B   Reviewing is the last stage of a personal development plan which involves re-assessing the time targets set and examining the needs to amend existing PDP or create a new PDP.

20   A   Downward communication follows the lines of authority of an organisation, that is, it flows from top to bottom.

21   C   Development is a long-term process of self-improvement. Training gives participants a specific skill set or knowledge base. Education is a lifelong process and comes from a number of sources including books, television, newspaper, family and friends.

22   B   Although recruitment and selection is one of the main responsibilities of an HR department, the department is not solely responsible for hiring a candidate. Most organisations also involve a manager or supervisor from the concerned department (where the job vacancy is) to participate in the recruitment and selection process.

23   C   Feedback and interaction takes place at each stage of training and development so that the process becomes more effective.

24   C   Procrastination is one of the barriers to effective time management. Procrastination occurs when an individual puts off doing work that he typically finds unappealing by finding distractions that are less important or productive.

25   B   Lateral formal communication represents the way employees from different departments, holding the same rank, communicate with each other through official or established channels of communication.

26   D   For communication to be effective, the message that a sender is sending should be clear, accurate and specific. It need not be creative.

27   C   The cluster effect represents the tendency of a reviewer to give all employees of a peer group the same rating regardless of their individual performances.

28   A   Development is a long-term process of self-improvement which involves identification and development of knowledge, expertise and skills in order to achieve long-term objectives.

SECTION F - RECRUITING AND DEVELOPING EFFECTIVE EMPLOYEES

SOLUTIONS TO MIXED QUESTIONS

1   ☑   Counselling represents the most common type of "on the job" training

      ☑   Counselling helps younger, less experienced employees on their career paths

Coaching represents the most common type of "on the job" training. Mentoring helps younger, less experienced employees in their career paths.

2   ⊙   A production manager sending a report to the purchasing manager outlining all the raw materials he would like to purchase.

Lateral communication represents the way employees communicate with employees (holding the same rank) from other departments.

3   ☑   Applying theory based principles in real life experiences

      ☑   Observing others' experiences before starting the activity

The first stage in Kolb's learning cycle is having an experience. The second stage is reflecting on the experience. The third stage is Interpreting and understanding the experience. The last stage is applying conclusions drawn from the experience in new situations.

4   ⊙   Identifying resources to perform tasks

5   ⊙   Person specification

A person specification describes the qualities necessary for a particular job. A job description includes details such as job title, job responsibilities, immediate boss and subordinates. A job analysis documents the requirements for a job.

6   ⊙   Tell and sell approach

In the tell and sell approach, the reviewer takes a judgemental approach by pointing out the employee's strengths and weaknesses, where he has met his targets and where he has fallen behind.

7

	True	False
The wheel pattern of communication is the slowest way of communicating	○	⊙
The chain pattern of communication is the fastest way to send a message	○	⊙

The circle is the slowest pattern of communication. The wheel is the fastest pattern of communication. The chain is faster than the circle pattern of communication.

8   ⊙   False

Effective training and development reduces the employee turnover by increasing employee commitment and satisfying the self-development needs of employees. Training and development also support transfers and promotions within the organisation so employees are encouraged to stay with the organisation.

9 ☑ Distorted content
☑ Selective interpretation

Distorted content typically occurs when a sender does not communicate directly with all intended receivers but uses intermediaries instead. Typically, some content of the message is lost or distorted when it is communicated from one intermediary to the next. Selective interpretation occurs when a receiver purposely interprets a message / information to suit his purposes.

10 ◉ The recency effect

The recency effect represents the tendency of some reviewers to base their appraisal on the most recent performance of the employee.

11 ◉ Learn through practically applying things taught

Pragmatists are individuals who enjoy theory and academic learning but only if the content of what is being taught can be applied to a practical or relevant situation.

12 ☑ Provides organisation with a wide source of candidates
☑ Easier to choose candidates on the basis of their seniority

Recruiting from within the organisation provides organisations with a limited source of candidates. It leads to a tendency for choosing candidates on the basis of seniority (time with the organisation) rather than suitability for a position.

13 ◉ False

The term time management refers to a set of tools and techniques that are used to plan and schedule an individual's time. Its main aim is to increase the efficiency and effectiveness of an individual in relation to how he uses his time.

14 ◉ Reflector

According to Honey and Mumford's learning styles, a reflector represents a person who likes learning by observing and then reflecting on what he has seen.

15 ◉ Coaching

During coaching, a more experienced employee or supervisor trains the employee on the requirements and functions of a particular job as well as on how to perform the various functions.

16 ◉ Competence test

A competence test assesses the level of knowledge and expertise a candidate has.

17 ◉ College campus

Sending recruiters to college and university campuses gives an organisation a chance to directly contact candidates that the organisation is interested in hiring. All the other options are indirect methods of recruiting.

18 ◉ Setting priorities

Setting priorities is one of the ways to improve time management. Prioritising tasks that need to be done is one method of ensuring that the most important work or activity gets done first and during the "best time". Failing to set priorities can be a barrier to effective time management.

19 ◉ The chain

In the chain pattern of communication each group member (or receiver) can only communicate with the person adjoining him. Therefore, the sender receives no feedback.

20 ☑ Relevant
☑ Timely

According to the SMART acronym, the objective needs to be Specific, Measurable, Attainable, Relevant and Timely.

F1- ACCOUNTANT IN BUSINESS

MOCK EXAM (Paper-based)

Time allowed: 2 hours

ALL FIFTY
questions are compulsory
and **MUST** be attempted

Do **NOT** open this paper until you are ready
to start the exam under exam conditions.

ALL FIFTY questions are compulsory and MUST be attempted

1   Helen is an enthusiastic woman and likes to immerse herself fully in new experiences. She likes to deal with practical problems and learn from hands-on experiences. She acts first and considers consequences later.

Which of Honey and Mumford's learning styles does Helen represent?

A   Pragmatist

B   Reflector

C   Activist

D   Theorist

(2 marks)

2   **Which of the following is not a reason for potential fraud in an organisation?**

A   Autocratic management style

B   Strategy of reward by results

C   Complex organisational structure

D   System of divided responsibilities

(2 marks)

3   The main difference in the roles of internal and external auditors is due to their relationship with the company and body to which they report to.

Is this statement true or false?

A   True

B   False

(1 mark)

4   A large multinational coffee manufacturing company has a policy of not allowing vending machines that sell its products to stock any other type of hot beverage.

This policy of the company is in response to which of the following competitive forces?

A   Threat of new entrants

B   Bargaining power of suppliers

C   Threat of substitutes

D   Competitive rivalry

(2 marks)

5   **In what order should the transactions for a credit sale take place if a sales control system is in place?**

A   Credit authorised, goods dispatched, order received, invoice sent

B   Order received, invoice sent, goods dispatched, credit authorised

C   Order received, credit authorised, goods dispatched, invoice sent

D   Invoice sent, credit authorised, order received, goods dispatched

(2 marks)

6   ABC Ltd is a major customer of XYZ Ltd. ABC follows XYZ's strategies closely, and actively pushes for reforms in its favour.

According to Mendelow's stakeholder mapping matrix which of the following statements is true?

A   ABC is a major customer, so XYZ should always try to keep ABC satisfied

B   ABC is already a major customer hence it falls in the minimal effort group for XYZ

C   ABC is a key player for XYZ, as it is one of the most important stakeholders of XYZ

D   Since ABC closely follows XYZ's strategies, XYZ should keep ABC informed about its strategies

(2 marks)

7 A company has an opening in its accounts department. The job title is accounts assistant, reporting to the accounts manager. The candidate's main role will be assisting the accounts manager and he / she will be responsible for making entries of the company's day-to-day transactions and keeping books of accounts. These details are called the _____.

Which two words correctly complete this sentence?

A   Job design

B   Job description

C   Job analysis

D   Job evaluation

(2 marks)

8 People tend to be more extreme in their decisions when they are in a group as opposed to a decision made individually. This tendency is called _____.

Which two words correctly complete this sentence?

A   Group polarisation

B   Group dynamics

C   Group effect

D   Group mechanism

(2 marks)

9 **Which of the following is an implication of a monetary policy for business organisations?**

A   An increase in the taxation level reduces the disposable income of individuals

B   An increase in government spending increases the demand for goods and services by the public sector

C   An increase in interest rates increases the price of borrowing and decreases demand for borrowing

(1 mark)

10 **Which of the following is not a characteristic of an informal organisation?**

A   Informal organisations that develop within an organisation are very active and dynamic

B   Informal organisations are very flexible in comparison to formal organisations

C   The 'Grapevine' is the most common by-product of an informal organisation which follows a specific hierarchy for informal communication

D   Informal organisations are spontaneous in nature

(2 marks)

11 Lorraine is working with Zeal Ltd. Her tasks include monitoring the working capital usage of the company, monitoring interest and foreign currency exchange rates and investigating, evaluating and selecting appropriate sources of project finance.

Which of the following finance functions best describes Lorraine's role?

A   Financial accounting and reporting

B   Financial management and treasury

C   Management accounting

D   Internal audit and control

(2 marks)

12 Susan was working as a sales manager in an organisation. She left the job as she wanted to move into the marketing field, in order to further her career. She has received some job offers for sales manager positions but she is searching for a suitable job opportunity in marketing.

What is this type of unemployment called?

A Structural unemployment

B Demand-deficient unemployment

C Seasonal unemployment

D Frictional unemployment

(2 marks)

13 **Which of the following statements about groups and teams is incorrect?**

A Both groups and teams can increase innovation and motivation

B Members of both groups and teams have individual accountability

C Group members share a common purpose whereas team members share a specific goal

D Groups work in an unstructured environment whereas teams work in a structured environment

(2 marks)

14 **According to Handy's 'shamrock' organisation model, which group of people in an organisation works within the role culture?**

A The professional core

B The contracted specialists

C The flexible workforce

(1 mark)

15 **Which of the following responsibilities should be included in the job description of an internal auditor?**

(i) Reviewing operational procedures

(ii) Reviewing the risk management practices

(iii) Making recommendations on improving internal control systems

(iv) Identifying and testing the operation of controls

A (i), (ii) and (iv) only

B (i), (ii), (iii) and (iv)

C (i), (ii) and (iii) only

D (ii), (iii) and (iv) only

(2 marks)

16 Rose conducted a performance appraisal for her assistant, Philip. During the appraisal Rose took the role of a judge pointing out Philip's strengths and weaknesses. She suggested areas of improvement for Philip and persuaded him to pursue an improvement plan.

Which performance appraisal technique has Rose used?

A Tell and listen approach

B Problem solving approach

C 360 degree approach

D Tell and sell approach

(2 marks)

17 **Which of the following is an example of an intrinsic reward?**

    A   Performance bonus

    B   Promotion

    C   Public recognition

    D   Self-esteem

    (2 marks)

18 **Which of the following is a function of a cash control system?**

    A   Restricting the authority to make payments

    B   Maintaining accurate records of banking transactions

    C   Ensuring payment and receipt of dues in time

    D   Authorising credit terms to customers

    (2 marks)

19 **Which of the following best reflects an economy in stagnation?**

    A   Rising inflation and balance of payments deficit

    B   Negative economic growth and full employment

    C   Declining GDP and rising prices

    D   Little or no economic growth and stable or falling prices

    (2 marks)

20 **Which of the following would an organisation consider when undertaking PESTEL analysis?**

    A   Productivity analysis

    B   Training needs

    C   Social trends

    (1 mark)

21 At the initial stage of its evolution the role of accounting was _____.

    Which of the following correctly completes this sentence?

    A   To report on the financial condition of the business

    B   To manage the working capital of the business

    C   To track and monitor the transactions of the business

    D   To record the financial information of the business

    (2 marks)

22 A multinational company has subsidiaries in three foreign countries. The VPs of each of these subsidiaries sent a report on the annual performance of each subsidiary to the CEO of the company.

    Which pattern of communication does this represent?

    A   The wheel

    B   The chain

    C   The Y

    D   The circle

    (2 marks)

23 Auditors use substantive tests to obtain audit evidence about the operating effectiveness of internal controls.

    Is this statement true or false?

    A   True

    B   False

    (1 mark)

24 Which of the following is **not** one of the principles recommended in the legislation for data protection and security?

    A   Personal data should not be excessive in relation to the purpose

    B   Personal data should be obtained only for a specified and lawful purpose

    C   Personal data should be deleted when unnecessary

    D   Personal data, once recorded, should never be amended

                (2 marks)

25 Which of the following is **not** an advantage of outsourcing for a company?

    A   Enables focus on the core competencies

    B   Better managerial control on the outsourced activities

    C   Increased productivity and better quality of outsourced activities

    D   Cost saving and economies of scale

                (2 marks)

26 Which of the following is an aspect of working capital management?

    A   Identifying the appropriate source of short-term financing

    B   Inventory reporting and valuation

    C   Verifying and maintaining non-current assets

    D   Monitoring the level of capital and long-term liabilities

                (2 marks)

27 Samuel works as a production manager in X Ltd. He pays attention to the needs and comfort of his team members, in the hope that this will increase their productivity. He always encourages a relaxed and friendly work environment in his team which often leads to a lack of direction and control. He assumes that his team members will work hard if they are happy.

Which style of leadership does Samuel represent on the Blake and Mounton managerial grid?

    A   5.5 Middle of the road style

    B   1.1 Impoverished style

    C   9.9 Team style

    D   1.9 Country club style

                (2 marks)

28 Computerised financial systems are less reliable than manual systems and too expensive over the long run.

Is this statement true or false?

    A   True

    B   False

                (1 mark)

29 Amenture is an organisation that campaigns and works to reduce the illiteracy rate in under-developed and developing countries.

What type of organisation is Amenture?

    A   Not for profit

    B   Non-governmental organisation

    C   Cooperative

    D   Public sector

                (2 marks)

30 Which of the following is a good "motivator" according to Herzberg?

A   Work

B   Pay and benefits

C   Relationship with peers

D   Job security

(2 marks)

31 The law relating to health and safety in the workplace states that a company should not allow any of its employees to use any machine without supervision.

Is this statement true or false?

A   True

B   False

(1 mark)

32 Employees at Oniel Ltd are governed by strict rules and laws which have been developed through different experiments and study of jobs and processes. Recently the management of Oniel realised that it needs to take into account the personalities of its employees as both individuals and as members of a group to increase their efficiency. It understood the fact that employees are not simply motivated by economic self-interest but have psychological needs.

The management of Oniel is moving to which school / theory of management thought?

A   The classical school

B   The human relations school

C   The scientific school

D   The pragmatic school

(2 marks)

33 An internal audit department has an opening for an internal auditor who will be responsible for analysing and evaluating business processes and providing recommendations to improve performance.

This opening is for which type of audit?

A   Transactions audit

B   Systems audit

C   Social audit

D   Operational audit

(2 marks)

34 The managing director of an organisation has five vice-presidents reporting to him. They are the VP production, VP marketing, VP finance, VP R&D and VP personnel. All the managers in the organisation report to these vice-presidents.

What type of structure does the organisation follow?

A   Functional

B   Matrix

D   Product

C   Divisional

(2 marks)

35 Which of the following does not regulate the accounting practices and financial reporting that organisations must follow?

A   Law

B   Stock exchange

C   Accounting bodies

D   Government

(2 marks)

36   Terry is a leader of a team assembled by his organisation. His team members are working independently and gathering information about each other. They are asking Terry lots of questions about the team norms, objectives, their roles and external relationships.

Terry's team is at which stage of Tuckman's theory of team development?

A   Norming

B   Storming

C   Forming

D   Performing

(2 marks)

37   Achievement belongs to the esteem needs in Maslow's "hierarchy of needs".

Is this statement true or false?

A   True

B   False

(1 mark)

38   A country is undergoing changes in the age structure of its workforce. Research shows that the number of elderly people in employment is increasing and in a few years' time there will be very few young working people.

Which of the following will cause an increase in the country's workforce?

A   Increasing birth rate and increasing mortality rate

B   Increasing birth rate and decreasing mortality rate

C   Decreasing birth rate and increasing mortality rate

D   Decreasing birth rate and decreasing mortality rate

(2 marks)

39   **Which of the following is not one of the main purposes of an internal financial control system?**

A   Ensuring compliance with all applicable laws and regulations

B   Ensuring the reliability of the financial reporting

C   Ensuring compliance with all applicable accounting standards

D   Ensuring safeguarding of assets

(2 marks)

40   Jenny is an efficient employee who is eligible for promotion. After getting engaged, she is denied promotion by her organisation on the grounds that she will not be able to provide the required commitment for the higher position after her marriage.

What Jenny's employer's act called in legal terms?

A   Unethical treatment

B   Indirect discrimination

C   Direct discrimination

D   Unlawful rejection

(2 marks)

41 **Which of the following is an advantage of committee decision-making over individual decision-making?**

(i)   Decisions involve compromise

(ii)   All decisions are recorded in minutes

(iii)   Better quality decisions

(iv)   Decisions have greater credibility

A   (i), (ii) and (iv)

B   (i) and (iii)

C   (i), (iii) and (iv)

D   (iii) and (iv)

(2 marks)

42 There is much documented research that downward communication is very often effective.

Is this statement true or false?

A   True

B   False

(1 mark)

43 SoftStance Ltd is a large IT company that emphasises teamwork and innovation. Each employee's performance is judged by results and each employee is a hands-on contributor to the company's success. There is no fixed corporate hierarchy and everyone has the ability to work in several areas.

According to Charles Handy's four cultural stereotypes, which type of organisation is SoftStance?

A   Zeus

B   Apollo

C   Athena

D   Dionysus

(2 marks)

44 **Who is primarily responsible for the prevention and detection of fraud in a limited company?**

A   Internal auditor

B   Board of directors

C   External auditor

D   Financial controller

(2 marks)

45 **Which of the following statements about business ethics is not true?**

A   Ethical responsibility extends to an organisation's shareholders and stakeholders as well as to society

B   Ethics involves a permanent commitment to abiding by a set of moral principles

C   There is no strong economic justification for organisations to behave ethically

D   Organisations need to consider their decisions in terms of both profitability and morality

(2 marks)

46 Sophia is an extrovert and a good networker. She explores new ideas and possibilities with energy and enthusiasm. She has the ability to develop contacts and negotiate with others on behalf of the team.

Which of the Belbin's team roles does Sophia represent?

A Team worker

B Plant

C Resource investigator

D Coordinator

(2 marks)

47 Which of the following is the last stage of the training and development process?

A Delivery

B Validation

C Design

(1 mark)

48 Which of the following systems would a company use for its personnel records, salaries, deductions and incentives?

A An office automation system

B A transaction processing system

C A management information system

D An executive support system

(2 marks)

49 Who is responsible for maintaining appropriate standards of corporate governance in a company?

A Board of directors

B External auditor

C Public oversight board

D Internal auditor

(2 marks)

50 Tom has been assigned the responsibility of guiding new joiners in his department on a range of activities to help them to understand their jobs and perform them efficiently. He trains them on the job under close supervision.

Which of the following describes the type of training given by Tom?

A Mentoring

B Counselling

C Instructing

D Coaching

(2 marks)

End of Question Paper

F1- ACCOUNTANT IN BUSINESS

SOLUTION TO MOCK EXAM

Do NOT turn this page until you have
completed the mock exam.

ACCA

1 **C** An activist represents the type of people who like to learn by doing. This type of people enjoys learning from methods such as on the job training.

2 **D** The system of divided responsibilities or segregation of duties helps to reduce the possibility of fraud. It becomes difficult for an employee to commit or conceal fraud, if his / her duties are restricted to a specific area. This is the core of the system of internal checks.

3 **B** The main difference between the roles of internal and external auditors is their purpose. An internal auditor is mainly concerned with adding value and improving an organisation's operations. An external auditor is mainly concerned with expressing an opinion on the financial statements of an organisation.

4 **C** Other hot beverages such as tea can be substitutes for coffee. The threat of substitutes depends upon the ease with which a customer can switch to an alternative product. The company is trying to limit customers' access to substitute products through its policy.

5 **C** In a credit sale transaction, the first step will be receipt of an order from a customer. Then, if the customer has a good credit rating, he will be granted credit. The next step is to dispatch the goods to the customer. Finally, an invoice is raised for the goods sold and this invoice is sent to the customer.

6 **C** ABC Ltd is a key player for XYZ Ltd as it has a high level of power and a high level of interest in XYZ. XYZ must pay attention to the needs of ABC.

7 **B** A job description includes details such as job title, overall purpose of the job, job responsibilities, candidate's immediate boss and candidate's subordinates.

8 **A** Group polarisation refers to the tendency of people to move towards a more extreme direction or be more extreme in their decisions when they are in groups. When confronted with a situation, the group as a whole typically has some overriding attitude towards the situation.

9 **C** At times of high inflation, an increase in interest rates increases the price of borrowing and decreases the demand for borrowing thereby decreasing the demand for goods and services.

10 **C** An informal organisation is flat and fluid with no hierarchies or fixed structure. A formal organisation has a hierarchical structure that allows authority and direction to flow from the top of the hierarchy to the bottom. Grapevine is a form of unofficial communication flow within the organisation. It hardly follows any hierarchical structure.

11 **B** The main finance and treasury functions within the business involve managing working capital, evaluating and obtaining finance and interest and currency exchange rate management.

12 **D** Frictional unemployment refers to a period during which able and willing individuals have left one job and are searching for another. It occurs due to difficulties in matching types of jobs with workers' skills or locations.

13 **B** In teams all decisions are usually reached by consensus and all team members are mutually accountable for the team's performance.

14 **C** According to Handy's 'shamrock' organisation model, the flexible workforce discharges part-time, temporary and seasonal roles. They perform routine jobs. They operate within a role culture as their roles are defined and discharged with clearly defined procedures. The role of this group is becoming important in contemporary organisations which are under pressure to reduce personnel costs.

15 **B** All the options stated are responsibilities of an internal auditor.

16 **D** In the tell and sell approach, the reviewer takes a judgemental approach which involves pointing out the employee's strengths and weaknesses, where he has met his targets and where he has fallen behind. The aim is to persuade employee to improve.

17 **D** Intrinsic rewards arise from carrying out the particular activity rather than any results that may arise out of completion of the activity. The other options are extrinsic rewards.

18 **A** A cash control system aims to put strict controls over cash payments to avoid malpractices such as fraud and theft. One such control is restricting the authority to make the cash payment to those who are authorised to make payments.

19 **D** Economic stagnation is said to occur when there is low or little economic growth and stable or falling prices. Growth of less than 2-3% per year is considered to be a sign of stagnation.

20 **C** In PESTEL analysis, S stands for social factors. Social factors represent changing consumer tastes and preferences and overall societal trends. Changes in social trends can have a great impact on business outcomes.

21 **D** The original role of the accounting function and the reason for its evolution is to record financial information on business transactions. This is still one of the main accounting functions.

22 **C** The Y pattern of communication is a derivative of the chain pattern. It has the disadvantage that its three groups / employees are completely isolated from each other.

23 **B** Substantive tests are used to verify the accounting figures and the accuracy of the financial information. Compliance tests are used to obtain audit evidence about the operating effectiveness of internal controls.

24 **D** The data protection and security legislation does not state this principle. It states that personal data should be kept up-to-date where necessary.

25 **B** One of the disadvantages of outsourcing is that it leads to loss of managerial control over the outsourced activities. It is more difficult for a company to manage external service providers than to manage its own employees.

26 **A** Working capital management refers to maintaining a level of capital which is sufficient to meet the cost of the organisation's operating requirements. Organisations need some form of working capital financing to cover periods where the organisation is waiting for payments to be received from customers but has to make payments to its suppliers,. This financing can either come from internal sources (past profits) or from borrowings.

27 **D** 1.9 Country club style has a high concern for people and a low concern for production. Managers using this style pay much attention to the needs of staff but little attention to achieving goals.

28 **B** Computerised financial systems are faster, more reliable and less expensive than manual systems over the long run. Although they are more expensive to implement than manual systems, they have much lower operating costs over the long term.

29 **B** Non-governmental organisations (NGOs) are any organisations that work towards a social, cultural, economic or educational cause.

30 **A** According to Herzberg, "motivators" represent factors that enrich an employee's job and therefore cause his motivation levels to increase. Work itself is one of the motivators stated by Herzberg. The other options are "hygiene factors".

31 **B** The law relating to health and safety at the workplace states three main precautions that organisations are required to take. These precautions are that all employees must be competent and trained, all machines and equipment must be safe and a safe working environment must be maintained at all times.

32 **B** The human relations school contends that social dynamics and group interactions directly affect the productivity and efficiency of employees. It states that employees also act as members of social groups and are motivated by complex psychological needs and values.

33 **D** Operational audit is concerned with auditing of business processes or operations. Its main objective is to appraise the effectiveness and efficiency of the organisation's activities and evaluate management's performance and its conformity with policies and budgets.

34 **A** A functional structure divides an organisation into the various functions that must be performed such as finance, marketing, production and administration. Each employee will then be assigned to one function or group.

35 **D** The law states the basic requirements that organisations must meet in relation to keeping and submitting proper records and preparing financial accounts. For a company to become listed on a stock exchange, it must fulfil certain requirements such as maintaining and reporting a high level and detail of financial information. Accounting bodies establish and monitor accounting and reporting standards The government does not regulate the accounting practices and financial reporting that organisations must follow.

36 C At the forming stage, a team is dependent upon a leader to guide and direct its activities. Individual members try to find out about each other and are usually unsure or unclear of their roles and responsibilities.

37 A Esteem needs represent an individual's urge to attain a degree of importance.

38 B An increasing birth rate means that there is a greater number of young people entering the workforce. A decreasing death rate means that there is a higher number of elderly people, some of whom will continue working. This will result in an increase in the country's workforce.

39 C Ensuring compliance with all applicable accounting standards is not the purpose of internal control systems.

40 C Direct discrimination is said to occur when a person is treated less favourably than others because of factors such as his gender, race or marital status.

41 D Greater quality of decision-making is accomplished, as committees draw on the knowledge, experience and skill sets of a group of people. Greater credibility is attached to the decisions reached by committees as they represent the viewpoints of a cross-section of people and not just one individual. Compromising on decisions is a disadvantage of committee decision-making.

42 B Downward communication is a one-way flow of communication with no means for subordinates to give their feedback or responses. This type of communication does not usually directly flow from a senior employee to junior ones but instead through intermediaries i.e. middle level employees.

43 C The Athena organisation represents a task culture which encourages a team approach. It promotes innovation and often gets the most out of employees. The emphasis is on results rather than procedures.

44 B The ultimate responsibility for preventing and detecting fraudulent practices and malpractices in a limited company is that of its board of directors. They are responsible for taking the necessary steps to prevent and detect fraud.

45 C Experience has shown that being ethical makes good business sense for an organisation in the long run since people are more willing to buy from, deal with or work for organisations that have an established reputation for behaving ethically.

46 C According to Belbin's team roles theory, a resource investigator is a very enthusiastic and extrovert individual. He / she focuses on negotiating for the team with outside parties and obtaining any resources the team may need.

47 B Once the training programme has been conducted, the last stage of validation is left to be completed. Here the success (or failure) of the training programme is evaluated.

48 B Transaction processing systems record and process an organisation's routine transactions. They enable personnel records to be maintained for each employee and a payroll to be maintained.

49 A Corporate governance is the system by which business corporations are directed and controlled by management. An organisation needs to maintain appropriate standards of corporate governance to ensure that managers, executives and the board of directors act in the best interests of the shareholders.

50 D Coaching represents the most common type of "on the job" training where a more experienced employee or supervisor trains the employee on what the job's requirements and functions are, as well as on how to perform the various functions.